Why Do I Keep Doing That
Why Do I Keep Doing That

Also by Dennis Wholey

The Courage to Change: Personal Conversations
About Alcoholism with Dennis Wholey

Are You Happy? Some Answers to the Most Important Question
*in Your Life (*released in paperback as *Discovering Happiness:*
Personal Conversations About Getting the Most Out of Life)

Becoming Your Own Parent: The Solution for Adult Children
of Alcoholic and Other Dysfunctional Families

When the Worst That Can Happen Already Has:
Conquering Life's Most Difficult Times

The Miracle of Change: The Path to
Self-Discovery and Spiritual Growth

Why Do I Keep Doing That

Why Do I Keep Doing That

Breaking the Negative
Patterns in Your Life

DENNIS WHOLEY

Health Communications, Inc.
Deerfield Beach, Florida

www.bcibooks.com

Library of Congress Cataloging-in-Publication Data

Wholey, Dennis
Why do I keep doing that? : breaking the negative patterns in your life /
  Dennis Wholey.
    p. cm.
    Includes index.
    ISBN-13: 978-0-7573-0582-5 (hardcover)
    ISBN-10: 0-7573-0582-2 (hardcover)
    1. Negativism.   2. Change (Psychology).   I. Title.
  BF698.35.N44W48 2007
  158.1—dc22

                                                              2006037038

Publisher: Health Communications, Inc.
            3201 S.W. 15th Street
            Deerfield Beach, FL 33442-8190

Cover design by Larissa Hise Henoch
Interior book design by Lawna Patterson Oldfield

For all the therapists, counselors, clergy, support groups, family, and friends who listen and give us hope, and for all of you who make the commitment and do the work necessary to change.

CONTENTS

ACKNOWLEDGMENTS

Every book requires the work and faith of many. This one has been a challenging and satisfying undertaking from concept to the bookmaking process to publication. It is a better book because these special people were involved.

At HCI I am particularly grateful to Michele Matrisciani, Peter Vegso, and Tom Sand for their belief in this book and especially to my editor, Andrea Gold, for her enthusiasm, insights, suggestions, patience, and coordination. Others at HCI who I would like to salute are Carol Rosenberg and Katheline St. Fort in the editorial department; designers Larissa Hise Henoch, Lawna Patterson Oldfield, and Andrea Brower in the art department; Kim Weiss in marketing; and Kelly Maragni, Sean Geary, and Lori Golden in sales.

A huge bundle of gratitude goes to agents Muriel Nellis and Jane Roberts of Literary and Creative Artists in Washington, D.C., for their commitment to the book, editorial guidance, warmth, and sensitivity to me as a writer and person. On their staff, I also want to thank Stephen Ruwe and Antonio Oppi for their day-to-day assistance.

Why Do I Keep Doing That? Why Do I Keep Doing That? utilized the varied talents and computer wizardry of Page Adams, who so accurately transcribed and typed many hours of taped conversations and essays and deciphered my handwriting, markings, edits, and rewrites. I thank Page not only for her abilities but also for her positive spirit, painstakingly performing a too-often unheralded task against impossible deadlines.

My friend Steve Lee worked ever so closely with me on the project over many months, making valuable and creative suggestions along the way and handling much of the electronic work involved in putting together the first assembled version of this very complicated mosaic.

That important work was continued by my friend Bill Trombley, who, in the homestretch, performed with skill, good humor, and patience the seemingly never-ending computer work that had to be executed in the later stages of the process to cut, paste, organize, edit, and submit the final manuscript.

I asked celebrated author Dr. Kay Redfield Jamison, professor of psychiatry at Johns Hopkins University, and writer, editor, reviewer Stephanie Abbott to read an early draft of the manuscript for confirmation I was on the right track. Their affirmation and input was needed at the time and accepted with gratitude.

Others who read an entire draft or some portions of the book in progress are Dr. Hamilton Beazley, scholar-in-residence at St. Edward's University; Rev. Ed Pritchard; Dr. Lisa Wholey; Bill Brockschmidt; Rick Taylor; Peter Roehrich; Cyrilla Barr; Jerry Cox, good friend and literary accomplice; and Elizabeth Cox. Thank you all for your willingness to invest your time, provide feedback, and offer encouragement.

At *This Is America,* I am grateful to our producer Jonathan

Oglesby, who is so generous with his many talents and skills. He has put forth extraordinary efforts toward this book and our weekly television series. I rely on his counsel, humor, dedication, and abilities. Jonathan continually goes many extra miles to support all of my projects. I treasure our association and working with him. Thank you as well to our willing and hardworking production assistant, Tim Abbondelo, for all the extras.

Past *This Is America* producers, Brian Eng and Ryan Black (the dynamic duo), gave extra time, comments, and support in the early stages of the work. I am ever so grateful to them.

A few others who also helped in many ways are Tarpley Long, M.S.W.; Hartvig Dahl, M.D.; Sis Wenger of the National Association of Children of Alcoholics; Midge Wholey; Rhoda Nary; Betty May; Birdie Pieczenik; Linda Mornell; Dr. David Spiegel; Nicole Johnson; Mike Anderson; Anthony Kim; Michael Nine; Chuck Harney; and longtime friends John Knight and Jeane Bice; and the Tuesday Night Group.

I am deeply grateful to all the professionals in this book, who trusted me, generously contributed to the project, and gave so freely their wisdom and experience. I am also indebted to those who have so honestly and inspirationally shared their personal stories.

Of course, I am grateful to my family, other friends, and business associates who have traveled this journey with me. Thanks for your interest, listening, encouragement, and love.

If I have left out anyone who contributed to this book and deserves to be acknowledged, I apologize. I always promise to make a "thank-you" list as the bookmaking process begins. I failed to do so, once again. Please accept my appreciation, and let me know of my omission so we can add you with gratitude in the next printing.

CONTRIBUTORS

Brad Blanton, Ph.D., has worked for more than twenty-five years as a psychotherapist in Washington, D.C. He is the author of *Radical Honesty: How to Transform Your Life by Telling the Truth* and conducts Radical Honesty Workshops throughout the country.

Nathaniel Branden, Ph.D., is the author of twenty books including the bestselling *Six Pillars of Self-Esteem, The Psychology of Self-Esteem,* and *Honoring the Self.* In addition to his private psychotherapy practice, he consults with business organizations on the use of self-esteem principles in the workplace.

Stephanie Brown, Ph.D., is the author of ten books and a founding board member of the National Association for Children of Alcoholics. She directs the Addictions Institute in Menlo Park, California, and is codirector of the Family Recovery Project at the Mental Research Institute in Palo Alto, California.

E. Virginia Demos, Ed.D., is assistant clinical professor of psychology at Harvard Medical School and member of the medical staff of the Austen Riggs Center in Stockbridge, Massachusetts.

Marylin Dyer Blair, M.A., is a career and job counselor, and owner, partner, and president of the Maryland Consulting Group. She holds a master's degree in human behavior, is a certified management consultant, and has more than twenty years experience in organization design and development.

Terence T. Gorski, M.A., is a lecturer, author, educational consultant, therapist, and the founder and president of the Center for Applied Sciences in Spring Hill, Florida.

Dean Hamer, Ph.D., is a molecular biologist and chief of the section on gene structure and regulation in the laboratory of biochemistry at the National Cancer Institute. He is the coauthor of *Living With Our Genes* and *The Science of Desire*.

Robert L. Johnson, M.D., is dean of the New Jersey Medical School, former president of the New Jersey State Board of Medical Examiners, and co-author of *The Race Trap*.

Peter D. Kramer, M.D., is a psychiatrist in private practice in Providence, Rhode Island, and is clinical professor of psychiatry and human behavior at Brown University. He is the author of the best-selling books, *Listening to Prozac, Should You Leave?, Moments of Engagement, Against Depression,* and *Spectacular Happiness.*

Lonnie MacDonald, M.D., is a psychiatrist in private practice in New York City specializing in the treatment of addictive disorders. He served as the first chief of community psychiatry at Harlem Hospital.

The late **Gerald G. May, M.D.**, is the author of many books, including *Will and Spirit, Care of Mind/Care of Spirit, Addiction and Grace, Simply Sane, The Dark Night of the Soul,* and *The Wisdom of Wilderness.* A psychiatrist and teacher, he was a senior fellow in contemplative theology and psychology at the Shalem Institute for Spiritual Formation in Bethesda, Maryland.

Pierre Mornell, M.D., is a psychiatrist in San Francisco's bay area and a consultant on hiring for Fortune 500 companies. He is the author of five books, including *Games Companies Play* and *Hiring Smart*.

Steve Pieczenik, M.D., is the first psychiatrist to have received a doctorate in international relations. He has over twenty years experience resolving international crises and hostage situations for the Department of State for four administrations. As a television producer and writer, he is co-creator of the *New York Times* bestselling Tom Clancy's Op-Center and Tom Clancy's Net Force books and television series.

Stella Resnick, Ph.D., is a psychologist in private practice in Los Angeles. She is a past president of the Western Region of the Society for the Scientific Study of Sexuality, and the author of *The Pleasure Zone: Why We Resist Good Feelings*.

Natalie Shainess, M.D., has worked as a psychiatrist and psychoanalyst for over fifty years. She has written over two hundred papers and professional book reviews, as well as the bestselling *Sweet Suffering: Woman as Victim*.

Scott Twentyman, M.D., is a psychoanalyst in private practice in Great Falls, Virginia, and a spokesperson for the Washington Center for Psychoanalysis.

Sharon Wegscheider-Cruse is the author of *The Family Trap, Understanding Me,* and *Learning to Love Yourself.* She is also the former president of Onsite Training and Consulting.

The past is never dead.

It's not even past.

—William Faulkner

CHAPTER ONE

THE QUESTION

My therapist used the phrase "the repetition compulsion" in our session one day. You've probably heard people say as I have, "When the student is ready, the teacher will appear." The teacher in my case was Tarpley Long, M.S.W., and I was ready.

It was the great Sigmund Freud (the father of psychoanalysis), she told me, who coined the term "repetition compulsion" after seeing unhappy clients in his office who were constantly complaining about some painful behavior or feeling—and then repeating it. Tarpley went on to explain that Freud believed human beings re-create in their adult lives the same dynamics—feelings, conflicts, and relationship styles—they experienced as children.

The purpose of this book is to explain why we all have this "compulsion to repeat"—and to varying degrees, we all do—and discover the most successful ways to stop doing what we don't want to do. There is a line between your past and your present, and if what is happening in your life now is not what you want it to be, the goal is to connect the dots and change your experience.

At Tarpley's suggestion I bought Freud's *Beyond the Pleasure Principle*. I'm intrigued by human behavior and found the subject matter fascinating. The book, which I read in a few hours, outlines three of Freud's core principles, which he felt motivated human behavior: the pleasure principle, the reality principle, and the repetition compulsion. (In his writing Freud uses the "repetition compulsion" interchangeably with the phrase "compulsion to repeat.") The three together explain in general—at least according to Freud—why we do what we do.

Freud believed our basic drive is to seek pleasure and avoid pain. Here's an example: Since humans are social animals, we avoid the pain of loneliness by being with others, often joining with a partner with whom we will be un-lonely. That in a nutshell is the "pleasure principle."

To explain behaviors he was observing in his patients that produced some stress and discomfort but were not debilitating, Freud created the "reality principle," which is analogous to our contemporary idea of "short-term pain, long-term gain." Saving money for retirement, going to college in order to get a better job, or taking tennis lessons to become a better player are simple examples of the reality principle in action.

The last core principle he identified was the "repetition compulsion," which is when people repeatedly perform the same negative actions. For example, a woman may be involved in her third relation-ship with an abusive partner. The behavior is pointed out to her, and she ends the relationship, only to later engage in yet another abusive relationship. For Freud, the question behind such behavior was "Why?"

It was this notion of "repetition compulsion" that struck a chord with me.

My Struggle

I am surprised I discovered the idea for writing this book while I was working on myself in therapy. I've always loved the saying, "You can sober up a drunken horse thief, but you still have a horse thief." I quit drinking out of necessity a long time ago, but I still had "issues," as people say today, which needed attention and work.

In my own therapy I was banging my head against a wall again—trying to make something happen that wasn't going to happen. This pattern kept appearing and reappearing in my life. It didn't make much difference if it had to do with personal or professional goals or relationships. They both involved situations that were not working out the way I expected, wanted, or occasionally demanded.

For those of you who know my history or have read my previous books, you will recall that I grew up in what professionals label a dys-functional home. My father was an alcoholic. He was a good man, but he was so focused on his own pain that he really didn't have much interest, energy, or time for anybody but himself. Consequently, I spent a lot of my life trying to get his attention in many ways: per-forming magic tricks in living room shows, playing golf (his sport, although I never saw him play or played with him), making first-string goalie on my high school hockey team (although I had never tried out for a sport before), and, I'm now convinced, becoming a television interviewer and host.

As an adult, I was looking for "love" in all the wrong places. For me, "love" translated to any kind of support, attention, approval, interest, validation, and affirmation—real or imagined. It was something that I desperately wanted.

Even the smallest nod in my direction prompted me to invest myself above and beyond the call of duty and reality, even when the overall message coming at me was "no" and the outcome I wanted clearly not in the cards.

No matter what the situation, professional goal, or personal relationship, the pattern was often the same. In my therapy sessions with Tarpley, we uncovered this repeating pattern of behavior, one that was causing me tremendous frustration and hurt, and we began to hold it up to the light for examination. I started to see that in business and friendships I sometimes chose poorly, or—to own my part in all of this—I ignored, dismissed, and discounted the negative signals coming at me, and kept trying to make them work.

In business, I sabotaged potential deals—one to the tune of one million dollars—or relentlessly pursued others that were obviously dead on arrival. Yet I went back to the well over and over again trying to make the impossible possible, just as I did when I was a kid.

In some personal relationships, I found myself hoping for more but feeling worthless, unimportant, and unlovable because of the lack of results I was getting. In many situations, in retrospect, my expectations were excessive and in some cases downright unrealistic.

In my adult life, I was duplicating the same dynamics with which I grew up. Difficult to see: yes. Hard to get a handle on: yes, yes. Possible to change: YES!

With hindsight, I can see that the fear of losing something or someone of value to me has on occasion caused me to hold on so tightly it may have caused others to flee. Through these real or imagined rejections I got to be the "victim"—a role I learned growing up, for sure. As you'll learn later on from Dr. Stella Resnick, a negative payoff is a "wonderfully clever" (my words, not hers) way of avoiding pleasure. Those dead-end friendships and relationships were (desirable?) ways of feeling bad and staying away from anything to do with the dreaded "I" word: intimacy.

There is a little saying that I like: "What other people think of me is none of my business." Well, yes and no. My self-worth is determined by what I do and me. On the other hand, how other people treat me personally and professionally is very much my business. Your actions toward me are my business. I read the signals more accurately today. If the lights are green, I keep moving forward. If the lights are yellow, I slow down. If the lights are red, I say, "Thank you very much. Next!"

The Question

The poet May Sarton told me that most nonfiction books were an attempt by the author to answer some burning question that wouldn't go away. Both Freud and I, it seemed, had one that wouldn't quit: Why do people repeat (over and over again) behaviors, relationships, and feelings that are clearly self-defeating, harmful, and painful?

That's the question Freud faced back then. It's the question that I took on as an author. It's the question we all face in our daily lives today.

How many of these following questions have you pondered?

Why does a person get into abusive relationships again and again?

Why do some people choose the wrong careers or take jobs they hate?

Why does a person keep getting fired?

Why do bosses hire employees who can't do the job?

Why is he always late?

Why is she so negative?

Why is he always sick?

Why does she always get drunk?

Why does someone who is sexually active practice unsafe sex?

Why do so many people struggle with money problems?

Why are so many of our friendships and intimate relationships so unfulfilling?

Why do we try so hard to get love from people who don't love us back?

How many people do you know who are "acting out" these negative behaviors? I know more than a few. And, how many times have you asked yourself, as I have: *Why do I keep doing that?* The answer seems to involve some variation of the repetition compulsion, and after reading Freud, I wanted to know more about it.

I consulted the Oxford Psychiatric Dictionary, which describes the repetition compulsion as "the blind impulse to repeat earlier experiences and situations quite irrespective of any advantage that doing so might bring from a pleasure-pain point of view." The entry goes on to say that Freud considered the repetition compulsion "more fundamental than the pleasure principle." It was the "more fundamental" phrasing that really hooked me.

According to the U.S. Surgeon General's office, 15 percent of the population—approximately 45 million Americans—are currently seeking professional mental health services for a conflict or illness which has created a level of "crisis" in their lives. With major exceptions—such as the death of a loved one, a job loss due to downsizing, incapacitating injury, physical disease, or severe mental illness—most of those in therapy or counseling, according to mental health professionals, are dealing with the compulsion to repeat some harmful, painful, or self-defeating behavior, feeling, or relationship.

Acting Out

Repetition compulsion can surface in a limitless number of ways. Maybe you can't stop eating. Maybe you are a workaholic, procrastinator, sex addict, or compulsive worrier. It could be that you're hurting, as Freud's patients did, from a pattern of failed relationships. On the other hand you might be a loner. It could be a feeling so powerful your life is controlled by it. Do you often feel fear, guilt, anger, or self-doubt so deeply that it affects everything you do?

We all have negative habits that we want to quit but can't. We try and we fail. Sometimes we seek out friends and family for advice and help. Other times, our shame is so great we keep our problem a secret. We make resolutions; we pray. We make a little progress, then often, and predictably, fall back into our old ways. When we are in desperate emotional pain, we may seek out psychiatrists, psychologists, therapists, counselors, clergy, coaches, or support groups. You may need some additional outside help yourself or may be getting it now.

Whatever your situation may be, I hope this book will assist you in ending the struggle, frustration, and self-criticism with which you are living, and lead you to the freedom and happiness which you desire and to which you have an absolute right.

Symptoms

As you read on, you will learn, as I have, that it really doesn't make any difference whether you drink it, smoke it, snort it, pop it, spend it, gamble it, eat it, work it, feel it, or have sex or a relationship with it—the compulsive habit, relationship style, or negative feeling you keep on repeating is actually a symptom. Your battle is probably not about one specific behavior or feeling either; it's more often about an overall pattern of negative "stuff" that probably shows up in many areas of your life.

As my sister Ann told me, Oprah Winfrey, who has had weight issues over the years, hit the nail on the head when she said to her trainer on her television program, "Oh I get it; it's not about the food." So the larger question becomes: "Why do I keep doing that?" What is at the heart of my workaholic nature, bad relationships, fear, anger, drug abuse, weight problems, or unsafe sex?

This book will explain why you compulsively engage in certain behaviors or feelings, and help you identify what's really going on in your life that is producing so much unhappiness. An intellectual and emotional understanding of why we do what we do can be the starting point for a healthy recovery. Hopefully the information and examples presented here will allow you to see what you are repeating from a different angle, help you to live your life differently, and encourage you to achieve a new level of happiness. Personally, I wish I had a lot of this information many years ago.

If you grew up with a great deal of stress, anxiety, and unhappiness, chances are that you have re-created it in your life today. What are you doing to keep up that stress, anxiety, and unhappiness today?

The Book

Freud, of course, introduced me to our topic, and my original idea was to put together a book proving that his repetition compulsion theory of a hundred years ago is just as valid today as it was then. In many ways I think it is. However, I've also learned that although Freud was groundbreaking in his thinking, the ideas and theories behind the repetition compulsion would evolve even in his own work.

One of the professionals I interviewed for this book, Nathaniel Branden, Ph.D., told me, "Don't look for one explanation to cover everything, because you won't find it. There may be a menu of possibilities." It was good advice for me, and it is good advice for us.

To help us understand the repetition compulsion, I've invited accomplished experts in many different fields of psychiatry, psychology, human behavior, and mental health to share their wisdom. These contributors have established and distinguished themselves over years of study, research, lecturing, and clinical practice. They hold various advanced degrees, have written bestselling books and scholarly articles, and have counseled tens of thousands of clients in various therapeutic disciplines. The wisdom and advice they offer here are from my many hours of conversations with them.

You'll also meet some extraordinary people like yourself—real examples of hope and inspiration—who will tell you about their personal battles with their own repetitive negative patterns and how they successfully conquered them. (You very well may bump into your own story on these pages, or perhaps it will jump out at you from between the lines.) They'll share their personal and very practical prescriptions for change and offer specific suggestions to help you overcome your own compulsion to repeat.

The material in this book is drawn from my own experience, print research, one of my previous books, interviews with the professionals, and essays from those who have "been there and done that."

I began all of my interviews with the professionals with the open-ended question: *Why do people repeat again and again behaviors, feelings, and relationships that are self-defeating, painful, and harmful?*

Here are some of the answers that surfaced:

Childhood programming

Parental expectations

Genetics/DNA

Low self-worth

Familiarity

Addiction

Avoiding pleasure

Conformity

Rebellion

Failed strategies

Satisfaction and gratification

Masochism

Mastery

As you contemplate your own behavior that is causing you frustration, stress, and suffering, one or several of these variations on the repetition compulsion theme may hit home.

While psychiatrists, psychologists, therapists, and counselors from varied disciplines often use different labels to describe repeating negative behavior patterns, most of these professionals agree that the majority of clients seeking their help are dealing with some piece of what Freud initially called the repetition compulsion. While some fascinating work in this area is being done in the fields of psychology and genetics, and new behavioral theories are under investigation as this is being written, professionals still agree that how we are raised as children is the single, most significant factor in how we value ourselves, how we navigate through life, and how happy we are as adults.

If you ask the average person why people repeat behaviors, relationships, and feelings that are clearly harmful, painful, and self-defeating, rather than pointing to deeper and actual causes, they often come up with answers such as:

Change is difficult.

The behaviors feel good.

They're familiar.

They fill a void.

They're comfortable.

We are creatures of habit.

The poet Edna St. Vincent Millay nailed it when she wrote, "It's not true that life is one damn thing after another; it's one damn thing over and over."

As you read this book, keep in mind that *Why Do I Keep Doing That?* is not a "how-to" self-help book. Change is not magically accomplished overnight in a few easy steps that you will discover in any book. But a book can help. Many have helped me.

We are creatures of habit, and while change can be difficult, it's also doable and well worth the effort. As you struggle with your own compulsion to repeat, it's important for you to know and accept:

- Whatever it is you are repeating does not make you a bad person, but it probably makes you feel bad.
- You are not alone.
- We all have our own compulsions to repeat.
- Others have changed and changed dramatically.
- You can change, too.

Throughout this book, you'll find questionnaires that will help you see the negative patterns in your life in a new light. Take a couple of minutes of quiet time to answer them as you read. Begin with the questionnaire on the following page.

1. Is there something going on in your life today that you want to stop but don't or can't? _____

   _____

   _____

   _____

   _____

   _____

2. Is that something a behavior, person, or feeling? _____

   _____

   _____

   _____

   _____

   _____

3. Have you asked yourself, "Why do I keep doing that?"

   _____

   _____

   _____

   _____

   _____

4. Do you beat yourself up when you do it again? _____

   _____

   _____

   _____

   _____

   _____

5. What word comes to your mind to describe your childhood?

_____

_____

_____

_____

_____

6. What were the negative behaviors in your family that caused your anxiety and unhappiness as you were growing up? _____

_____

_____

_____

_____

_____

7. Is there a recurring negative feeling that you experience today, which you experienced back then?_____

_____

_____

_____

_____

_____

8. Have you "chosen" someone to be in your life today who disappoints you, lets you down, or asks too much of you?

_____

_____

_____

_____

9. What do you want to change in your life? _____

   _____

   _____

   _____

   _____

   _____

10. What are you willing to try to do differently than you've tried in the past? _____

   _____

   _____

   _____

   _____

Let's get started.

CHAPTER TWO

THE REPETITION COMPULSION

To learn more about the compulsion to repeat, I met with Dr. Scott Twentyman in his Virginia office.

———

Scott Twentyman, M.D.

IS A PSYCHOANALYST IN PRIVATE PRACTICE IN
GREAT FALLS, VIRGINIA, AND A SPOKESPERSON FOR
THE WASHINGTON CENTER FOR PSYCHOANALYSIS.

Dr. Twentyman generously gave me an introductory lesson in Freud 101, underscoring for me that Freud's theories and Freud himself were really works in progress. Although controversial back then and maybe even more so today, most people won't deny that the fields of psychiatry and psychology we know today had their roots back in Vienna with Freud. Dr. Twentyman explained:

"The clinical definition of repetition compulsion is a repeating pattern of behavior in a person's life—at least a significant portion of which he or she is not aware—that is causing some degree of difficulty for that person. The reasons for it lie outside of awareness as well.

"Unconscious repressed feelings drive our thinking and behavior. It's like an iceberg where nine-tenths is outside of conscious awareness. That's not always a bad thing. Certainly, that's where our conflicts reside, but it's also where our intuition and creativity come from. There's a tendency to equate unconscious with bad and conscious with good. That's an oversimplification. My belief is that most of our life is outside of conscious awareness, but I also think that's part of what gives us its richness.

"Freud believed that, if we have an unacceptable impulse, we get rid of it through repression—pushing it outside of conscious awareness. We have a desire but have a conflict around the desire, so we repress it. Yet the desire keeps trying to get expressed, so it might come out in a disguised form. That would be a symptom, which would both hold the desire at bay and yet gratify it a little bit at the same time."

Dr. Twentyman offered the classic example of sexual desire: A person who is in conflict about desire represses it. Yet the desire, which still needs to be expressed, is expressed by way of a symptom. For example, perhaps because of a very conservative or religious background, the person has feelings of guilt about that sexual desire. Consequently, the behavior—the symptom—to deal with the conflict may be anything from overeating or alcohol abuse, to a failed relationship or being a workaholic.

"Freud's thinking was to bring the conflict into awareness, and then you could deal with it rationally. Make the unconscious conscious and that should do it. The only problem was that when he did that, he found his patients kept on doing whatever it was they were doing. Bringing it to the patient's awareness didn't make the conflict go away.

"Freud had a couple of problems about what was going on and how to explain it. People were engaged in doing harmful behaviors that were bringing them unhappiness. He thought, 'My theory says these problems are caused by the behavior being unconscious, and if you make it conscious, the problem goes away. What I see in my consultation room is that I point these things out to people and they say, "Yes, I see that," and then they do it again.'

"So, he had not only a clinical problem but a theoretical problem as well. He has his model of how the mind works—that we seek pleasure and avoid displeasure or pain—but how do you account for the clinical observation that you've got people who seem to be seeking out pain? They keep getting involved in destructive relationships or repeating destructive behavior. That doesn't line up with the pleasure principle and that doesn't line up with the reality principle either. What's going on?"

I asked Dr. Twentyman what Freud's answer was to this question.

"People have a compulsion to repeat self-destructive behavior over and over again. Almost by definition, a compulsion is something you feel you have to do, whether it makes sense or not. If you resist it, you feel a great deal of distress. You have to do it.

"I've seen people who were compelled to make unwise business decisions or get into unwise business deals, and it cost them dearly. I've seen people get involved with partners that any reasonable person could see they should avoid. I've seen people make extremely unwise investment choices in speculative stocks, having a need to hit a home run or be a big shot. They do it again and again. There may be a need to validate low self-esteem, saying, 'See, I really am worthless.' That gets into a complicated area involving how people see themselves and a lot of that comes from the kind of messages they got growing up. It can really be astonishing how carefully people can arrange to create difficulties in their lives."

Mastery

Dr. Twentyman offers some thoughts on the challenges he faces as an analyst and the potential rewards and benefits for the individual in treatment.

"Some psychoanalysts think that what the person is trying to do is master some conflict that he or she is experiencing. Perhaps each time a person repeats the behavior, he learns something from it, or with the help of an analyst, sees some aspect of it not seen before. It's not enough to just point it out to a person once; you have to point it out again and again and again. With enough repetition, individuals gradually get hold of the conflict and become fully aware of all of the different ways that it interweaves throughout their life, and the problem's solved.

"For example, a woman who marries an alcoholic and who gets divorced may turn around and marry another alcoholic or a compulsive gambler or somebody who beats her. Now if you look carefully you'll see this pattern extends further than that. She has these relationships but then she'll get into a job where there's a demanding and sometimes downright abusive boss. And then she gets involved with friends who take advantage of her or treat her badly. You'll see that same pattern in a whole variety of areas of her life.

"What's good about the 'working through' approach is, you see clinically that individuals will have a growing awareness of why they're repeating a particular pattern or behavior and all the different ways it comes up in their lives."

Dr. Twentyman cautions against focusing on only the symptom:

"Everybody who comes into therapy has a significant reason for being there. If you see the problem as an expression of something going on with the whole person, then you're more able to see aspects of the repetition compulsion that somebody else might miss if they're just focused on a specific symptom. The repetition compulsion is the behavior that's identifiable, but it's symptomatic of something that's bigger.

"The reason it's a symptom is that it's a pattern that got established when the person was a child and didn't have a lot of resources for coping. So the person developed the best solution with what was available at the time. It worked for them then, but now it doesn't work so well."

If as a youngster you were always the one to crack jokes to ease family tension, that technique may have served you and your family well back then. However, an excessive use of humor in professional situations and adult personal interactions can backfire. The person on the receiving end may feel she is personally being discounted or that what she is trying to say is not being listened to at all.

As youngsters we adapt to dysfunctional family situations and adopt "survival" strategies that work in our childhood environments but may cause us difficulty in the outside world later on. The outside world doesn't play by the same rules as our family, but if these strategies are all that we know, they're what we'll use.

Everyone—those you think you know well, those you watch from afar, those you read about or watch on television—is struggling to some degree with their own version of the repetition compulsion. The more difficult the past, the more difficult the present.

Meet Victoria, a thirty-four-year-old sales rep for a major clothing chain based in Los Angles. Everyone sees her as a caring, giving, selfless person.

Victoria's Compulsion: People Pleasing

"When I was growing up, nobody really took care of me, so I never learned to take care of myself. We found out later on that my mother was a prescription drug addict. I just thought she was depressed all the time, and I guess she was. She had no energy, complained a lot, and would spend days upon days in bed. She actually overdosed once after I went off to college and ended up in the hospital. She recovered, thank God, and finally got off the painkillers. However by that time, her change of behavior was too late to have any real positive impact on me. The damage had been done.

"My dad never seemed to be around. He'd tell us it was his 'crazy job at the newspaper,' but I always thought that he had a girlfriend on the side. So my sister and I spent our time as kids going to school and waiting on my mother. I learned how to take care of her—and other people—real good.

"Mom was often in a stupor and came across as drunk so we never invited any of our school friends to come over to our house. We were too embarrassed. In a way we kind of had an absent mother because of her drug use and an absent father because of what he said was his work.

"One night in a long rambling phone call I complained to my sister that I felt my boyfriend was taking me for granted. She sent me a book she'd read by Pia Mellody and Andrea Miller called *Facing Codependence*. Pia Mellody started a center in Arizona called The Meadows, which offers short-term workshops for people like us who had difficult childhoods and were living unhappy adult lives. One of Pia's weekends is called 'Survivors.' That registered with me. Although I think they use the term survivors as a compliment, I felt that I wasn't really living, I was just surviving.

"Pia Mellody's mantra, my sister told me, is 'Ask for what you need; ask for what you want; and listen to what you get.' That phrase hit home with me big time. I thought about the people in my life— there really weren't that many—and I realized that I never asked for what I wanted and needed. As far as listening to what I got, that's all I did—listen—and what I was getting was everybody's problems. No one was asking me how I was doing, who I was, what were my hopes and dreams and fears, what did I want to do.

"After I finished reading that book, I joined a codependency support group and those meetings made my head hurt. Week after week I'd leave the meetings in shock, thinking of how much I neglected myself by literally serving others. I learned—just by listening to other people talking about their lives in those meetings—that my relationships really weren't relationships at all; they were all one-sided. I was a one-person support group.

"That was true of my boyfriend, my two girlfriends, the people I hung out with at work, and even my boss. It pained me to admit that I had made their lives more important than my own and that I had built a circle of people around me who, by their actions or inactions, didn't really care about me very much at all. It was all about them. I am embarrassed to even say this too, but my whole life was wrapped up—or trapped—in taking care of emotionally needy and sick people, just as I had done with my mother when I was young. What I discovered was I was sicker than all these people around me.

"About six months into those codependency meetings I began to change. A few in the group would go out for coffee and dessert every week after the meeting and invited me to join them. I began to develop relationships with a couple of them, relationships that were a whole lot healthier and more equal. I was real uncomfortable in the beginning, but I fumbled my way along. One of them suggested therapy and I found a good therapist who really held my hand through a lot of anger and tears.

"I stopped being a doormat at work and even took a few months emotional vacation from everyone to rebalance myself and set some boundaries about listening to other people's problems. That was hard. I had to learn to live with me. I cleaned house. I hope that this doesn't sound cruel, but I fired my boyfriend. To say he was a slacker would be charitable. He was really living off me.

"I can slip back into old patterns. I'm attracted to a certain type of person. But nowadays I catch myself quickly. I don't think relationships have to be fifty-fifty every day, but they've got to balance out over time. 'Your wish is my command' is no longer the price of admission into my inner circle today.

"Over the past year, I've developed some self-respect and self-esteem. I know what I need. I'm working on knowing what I want. I'm attracting a whole different kind of person today. I'm pretty happy and I have some really supportive friends. It's taken a lot of work, but it sure has been worth it."

WHY DID I KEEP DOING THAT?

"Looking back on it now, it seems to me that I always hooked up with people who needed someone to take care of them. Maybe I was sending out some signals along those lines, because needy people certainly found me. I never really knew what I wanted or needed but I sure as hell knew what they wanted and needed. I came, I gave, I listened to their problems. Just as I took care of my mother as a kid, I took care of everyone around me as an adult. My mother came to me in many disguises. I'm embarrassed to say that taking care of other people made me feel better about me—and even *better than* them."

My Suggestion for Change

"If someone came to me today with a story like mine, I'd direct that person to the Internet and suggest she or he Google 'codependency characteristics.' A few of them that hit me in the gut are:

My good feelings about who I am stem from being liked by you.
My mental attention is focused on you.
My self-esteem is bolstered by solving your problems.
I am not aware of how I feel. I am aware of how you feel.
My fear of rejection determines what I say or do.

"If those characteristics resonate with you, you belong at codependency meetings. Do yourself a favor and commit to a dozen meetings. At the end of that time, if you don't think you belong, they will gladly refund your misery."

Problems Are Sources of Information

According to Dr. Twentyman, "Regardless of what brings a person into therapy, at least some part of it can be viewed in the context of the repetition compulsion," and his explanation for this complex human behavior is powerful in its simplicity:

1. The behavior is an expression of a conflict.

2. The conflict is an attempt at solving a problem.

3. The hidden conflict is driving the behavior.

4. The compulsion is creating the problem and is also relieving some stress.

5. The behavior is actually a symptom, and it's a solution that doesn't really work.

Dr. Twentyman concludes:

"Using the term repetition compulsion or understanding the concept on an intellectual level isn't what's key. What's essential is knowing or believing that there's a lot of your life outside your awareness that affects what you do. The more awareness you have, the more control you have over your life.

"Try to turn problems into sources of information. The problem is telling you that there's something wrong. It's a signal to you that something needs tending to, needs to be understood, and needs to be worked on. Instead of thinking about problems in terms of how to completely eliminate them, use them as keys to a more satisfying life.

"A lot of time, when people come in to see me all they want is to make the pain go away. They're missing out on what that pain is telling them. That's throwing away something of exceptional value.

"Self-awareness is a good thing. Ultimately, it comes down to how curious you are about your inner life. How willing are you to explore it? That's true whether you're in therapy or not. You have to have curiosity about yourself."

If you are banging your head against a wall right now, you might ask yourself:

- What is this negative thing I keep doing?

- How often has this happened?

- What role do I play in it?

- Why do I keep doing that?

While there are external events in life over which we have no control, if there is something negative going on in your life now, you have to own the fact you play a part in it. However, it's crucial to keep in mind: "I am human, everyone makes mistakes, I cannot be perfect, I'm not alone, others have changed, I can too."

CHAPTER THREE

COMFORT ZONES AND SELF-WORTH

We all have a comfort zone; and for the most part, that's where we live—same people, same home, and same friends. Some people will live and die with the television set tuned to NBC, and if your folks used Colgate toothpaste and voted Republican, chances are you will too. We are, indeed, creatures of habit.

The friends you have, the car you drive, the clothes you wear, the work you do, the money you make, the person you call your mate or best friend all say volumes about you and your comfort zone. Accept it or not, your comfort zone was created a long time ago and for the most part that's where you live.

Healthy parents communicate two vital messages to their children: *"You are good, lovable, capable, worthwhile, and important,"* and *"Life is challenging, yet an exciting and fun place to be."* If these positive messages are learned during childhood, we will be able to navigate successfully through the ups and downs of adulthood, handle whatever we encounter along the way, and enjoy the experience and adventure of life.

Childhood Programming

To understand more about how our childhood experiences shape our adult skills, I talked to Dr. Robert L. Johnson.

Robert L. Johnson, M.D.

IS DEAN OF THE NEW JERSEY MEDICAL SCHOOL,
FORMER PRESIDENT OF THE NEW JERSEY STATE BOARD
OF MEDICAL EXAMINERS, AND CO-AUTHOR OF *THE RACE TRAP*.

Dr. Johnson takes us back to our beginnings and tells us how childhood programming works.

"In early childhood, we all learn how to behave in a variety of situations. We learn how to walk. We learn how to talk. We learn how to dress ourselves. We learn how to react to persons of the same sex and how to react to persons of the opposite sex. The most important things we see, learn, and experience are those done by individuals who are most significant in our lives, usually our parents or siblings.

"In my work with parents I tell them how critical it is to make sure they behave as they would want their children to behave as adults. What they do when their children are one, two and three years of age will affect how their youngsters are going to be when they're sixteen, seventeen or eighteen. It's an enormous burden on parents to be aware of what they're doing and how they're doing it may affect their children."

Dr. Johnson stresses that our behavior lessons come not only from parents but also from our siblings and other significant individuals as well.

"I have two little nephews who are separated in age by a year. Recently, at a family gathering, the three-year-old came over to the adults and hugged them. The two-year-old was looking at him and then did exactly the same thing. He was learning behavior. For him, whatever his older brother does is going to be very important. Interestingly, my nephews' father is in a similar situation with his younger brother. They're in their late twenties. They both have the same appearance, and I noticed at one point that both were scratching their heads the same way. They mirrored each other in their behavior. I'm sure the younger one learned it from the older one."

Anyone in the household or anyone who is a significant part of a child's formative years will play a role in developing the child's comfort zone. If a child is raised in a loving home, odds are that as an adult, he or she will have a high level of self-esteem, which will translate to a healthy comfort zone. Odds are favorable that these adults will seek out positive and affirming relationships. As emotionally healthy and socially skilled adults, they will choose as their significant others and friends those who also have their feet on the ground and are comfortable living life on life's terms.

An ongoing debate in our country centers around the effectiveness of parenting in homes in which both parents work or in single-parent homes.

Since parents are key to the child's future positive or negative comfort zone, Dr. Johnson responds to some obvious and normal concerns.

"The existence of a two-parent family or even a mother who stays at home does not guarantee that problems don't occur. I emphasize that it's the quality of parenting. Both mother and father may be home, but they may not spend much time with their children. Father may come home and sit in front of the television and not even talk to the children, and mother may have a thousand things to do. They may spend time with their children, but yet they don't really communicate with them. On the other hand, parents who are both working may be so attuned to their situation they may compensate and spend extra quality time with the children and that may end up being more beneficial.

"Most people would say that their children need both male and female influences in order to develop. However, it's certainly possible that a single parent may be able to supply both types of input. Influences don't necessarily have to come from the parents, but they need to come from somewhere. Children will generally find them somewhere in their environment."

Children can also be influenced in other ways. Everything from ethnic heritage to birth order can affect a child. Today, Dr. Johnson tells us, many people worry about the effects of our present-day American culture on children:

"In this country, we worry a lot about how influences outside the family affect children. While movies, television, and music certainly have some effects, they pale in comparison to the effects of the family.

It is my observation that the extent to which influences outside the family such as the media and peers are able to affect a child is dependent upon the quality of parental teaching and quantity of time spent with parents. In other words, if parents are around they easily compensate for whatever is on television. If the parents are not around, negative outside factors may indeed exercise greater influence."

While nurturing is critical, there are influences of nature governing us as well. I've learned a bit about genetics because of my writing on chemical dependency. I understand that there is a genetic predisposition to depression, happiness, sexual orientation, and obesity. However, it never occurred to me that we could be "wired" to do what we do in so many other areas—including the repetition of negative behaviors. In the nurture versus nature debate, both can be at work determining our behaviors, feelings, and relationships. This information is essential to growing our knowledge about behavior.

Genetics and DNA

To find out how genetics determine our behavior, I talked to Dr. Dean Hamer.

Dean Hamer, Ph.D.

IS A MOLECULAR BIOLOGIST AND CHIEF OF THE SECTION ON GENE STRUCTURE AND REGULATION IN THE LABORATORY OF BIOCHEMISTRY AT THE NATIONAL CANCER INSTITUTE. HE IS THE CO-AUTHOR OF *LIVING WITH OUR GENES* AND *THE SCIENCE OF DESIRE*.

Dr. Hamer begins with some interesting observations about the genetic factors at play in self-directed (high-esteem) and other-directed (low-esteem) people—and the consequences of DNA.

"There are people who are able to adapt their behavior to accommodate whatever their own goals and values are. If they want X, then they will do Y to get it. They rely on themselves. They feel like they have a purpose in life, and they do whatever is necessary to achieve that end. It's really all a matter of what personality psychologists sometimes call self-directedness, also commonly referred to as self-reliance or even self-esteem. People who are not self-directed are just the opposite. They tend to do things in reaction to outside forces, what other people want, or circumstances that envelop them at the moment. They continue to do the same behaviors even when it's not achieving what they want or even when it's not consistent with their own value system. They're low on self-reliance and they generally tend not to think very highly of themselves because they frequently don't attain what they want. Self-directedness is about 50 percent genetic. We now can identify one of the genes and we have some idea of how it operates."

Dr. Hamer explained to me the importance of this gene for the serotonin transporter. Serotonin, an important molecule in the brain, has a big effect on people's mood and emotions. It's a target for anti-depressant drugs such as Prozac, Zoloft, and Paxil. That gene for the serotonin transporter varies from individual to individual. It can work very effectively in some people and less so in others. People with a well-working form of the gene, according to Dr. Hamer, are more self-directed. People with a poor-working form of the gene are less self-directed. He says, "It's just an inborn part of a person's temperament."

Dr. Hamer goes on:

"Feeling bad about the world and feeling bad and sad about yourself translates into an inability of people to do the things they need to do in order to feel better about themselves. The people who tend to be more self-directed have a higher level of serotonin, so they're less likely to engage in negative behavior. It's important to realize that all of the brain chemistry is a two-way street. For example, one can be born with a gene that makes one's serotonin low, but it is possible to change one's brain serotonin levels by doing things that make you happy or at which you are effective. So, people's behavior is not predetermined.

"There is a lot that people can do to change behavior and thereby change their brain chemistry. However, one's inborn DNA genetic makeup does tend to tilt the scales and make it easier or more difficult for some people to change than it is for others."

Dr. Hamer concludes with this amazing thought.

"All of the addictive behaviors, whether for drugs, alcohol, gambling, sex, perhaps even shopping, have a substantial genetic component. In addition to a predisposition toward anxiety or depression, there might also be a predisposition toward the repetition of negative behaviors. The same brain chemical, in fact, is related to depression, anxiety, and bad habit formation."

Self-Esteem

Self-esteem plays a dominant role in determining our comfort zone. Esteem is the value you place on yourself, and most of it was formed by the messages you got or didn't get when you were a child—messages that were overtly, covertly, consciously, subconsciously, directly, or indirectly given by your parent(s), siblings, and others who were directly involved in your upbringing. High self-esteem gleaned from positive messages translates to feeling good about yourself and feeling up to handling whatever life throws your way.

Sharon Wegscheider-Cruse

IS THE AUTHOR OF *THE FAMILY TRAP, UNDERSTANDING ME* AND *LEARNING TO LOVE YOURSELF*. SHE IS ALSO THE FORMER PRESIDENT OF ONSITE TRAINING AND CONSULTING.

Sharon Wegscheider-Cruse defines self-worth and the negative consequences when it's lacking.

"Self-worth is *the* basic personal need. Self-worth is understanding, accepting, loving, and believing in yourself in order to have the courage to make choices and changes. Self-worth entails how we feel about ourselves, how we teach others to treat us, and how we set boundaries and limits to ensure that we have nourishing lives emotionally, physically, and spiritually."

Meet Manuel. Manuel is a twenty-five-year-old alumnus from a prestigious Ivy League university who has been struggling since he graduated three years ago to "find himself" and establish a rewarding career path. He is bright, possesses a wicked sense of humor, and embodies a street-smart style. I asked him to create a title for his testimonial. He calls it, "Liking the Guy Looking Back at Me in the Mirror."

Manuel's Compulsion:
Self-Doubt

"When I grew up, there was a large rift internally between my family and me, and I felt alone. Externally, I was the perfect little kid, but I had constant feelings of sadness. Blame it on witnessing first-hand my parents' broken marriage, feeling like the odd kid out in school, or being raised in a conservative family where 'rights' and 'wrongs' were heavily stressed.

"At times, I honestly felt that the world would not care if I were gone. Luckily, when it came to the few times I seriously considered suicide, I knew deep in my gut that I just couldn't go out that way. I wasn't going to be 'that guy.' Besides what if I could make a difference?

"However, there was one trap that I fell into when I decided to believe in my future and myself. I somehow came to the conclusion that my only purpose was to amass large sums of money. I formed an unhealthy correlation to the amount of money that I had in my pocket to my attitude toward that guy in the mirror. I figured that if I had money everything would be okay. People would like me, I would have power, and people would respect me for having what they didn't. Oddly enough, when I had a lot of money, I became arrogant and closed. When I had none of it, I was embarrassed, felt stupid and alone."

"I'm in the process of breaking the strong connection between the opinion I have of myself and the money I have in the bank. I've also set a goal to allow people into my life without expecting anything from them. There have been some setbacks along the way, where I have made some bad investments and shut some people out, but those experiences have given me a chance to reflect and regroup.

"I have come to the understanding that I am responsible for my own thoughts, and if I don't like the thoughts floating around in my head it is up to me to change them. I have noticed that often when I am feeling down it's because I am physically alone at home or in my car.

"Nowadays, when my mind wanders and gets the better of me, I call people and I make dates to hang out together. It's nothing grand, but bouncing my struggles off friends really helps relieve some of the tension that I create from thinking too much.

"I enjoy reading and for a change of scenery, I will often go to the local bookstore. There's a lot more energy in the store than at home when I am alone. Besides, since I live in a relatively small town, I never know who I'll meet there. Going out ensures that I'm not going to sit around in my pajamas.

"One of my favorite things to do is to go biking or jogging. The physical exercise is great for me, and I find that it clears my head too. I can feel the difference on days that I ride or run and days when I don't. I am by no means a great athlete, but getting the blood flowing and the heart pounding helps me release some of those negative feelings and stop the self-doubting inner talk. I've also been trying meditation to help calm my mind, and I have a collection of inspirational tapes by Napoleon Hill, Thomas Willhite, and Jim Rohn that I listen to while I'm driving, riding on the subway, or late at night when I'm trying to fall asleep.

"I have also been going to personal-growth seminars that have helped me break the pattern of associating my self-worth with my net worth as well as conquering my solitary tendencies. I've learned more about myself, shared experiences with others, and found out what makes people tick. This is especially true when we discuss things that have nothing to do with money.

"I'm beginning to see that we're not all that different on the inside. We all want the same basic things—to love and be loved, make a difference, and achieve some level of peace, happiness, or satisfaction. It is with this understanding that I can look at other people and say, 'That guy is not much different than I am. He may look different, talk different, and act different, but we're just two dudes.' I can also look at the people I associate with and know that since we're all pretty similar, our ups and downs must be pretty similar. So instead of going about my struggles alone, I actively ask my friends if they understand what I'm thinking and talking about. Chances are they do and it's getting easier to open up to them. I'm learning to enjoy the process and include others on my journey. It hasn't happened overnight, but the 'light' at the end of the tunnel is getting closer.

"Today I can tell you for sure that I matter and there are people that care for me. And I do make a difference."

In order to numb ever-present and painful feelings of worthlessness, we often fall into the miasma of addiction. All addictions make us feel good temporarily and kill painful feelings. They also block out reality and that spells trouble. Sharon Wegscheider-Cruse explains:

"Symptoms of low self-worth are feeling overly responsible, busyness, workaholism, a tendency toward addictive relationships, and self-abusive addictions such as overeating, anorexia, drug dependency, alcoholism, nicotine addiction, and relationship dependency. I call it a 'deathstyle' instead of a lifestyle."

We also pay a horrible price in our quest for value when we seek it from others. The character Grace, on the television show *Will & Grace*, sadly has it all wrong when she asks bewilderedly, I recall, "How are you supposed to know how you feel about yourself, if you don't know what others think about you?" That's other-esteem. Ms. Wegscheider-Cruse spells out the price we pay:

"Without a sense of self-worth, we need to get the approval of others, need to keep up an image for others and respond to the demands of others. We live an other-directed life, which means to completely lose touch with who we are. We have grown up in a culture in which many children, especially children who have come from any kind of a painful home, have learned to monitor what's expected of them instead of what is happening to them.

"We learn not to be angry, not to get too excited or silly, not to have trust or hope. We get serious and controlling about things. When we do that we get further and further away from who we really are. We're dependent on others, and if we have to depend on other people to tell us we're worthy, then we have to fit in to what those other people want.

"Are we doing it right? Do we ever do it right enough? Are we doing enough of it? Do we look right? Do we talk right? Do we act right?

"We become other dependent. Then we become relationship dependent, work dependent, success dependent, and chemical dependent. We get caught up in a variety of self-destructive behaviors."

The Circle of Fear

———

Lonnie MacDonald, M.D.

IS A PSYCHIATRIST IN PRIVATE PRACTICE IN
NEW YORK CITY SPECIALIZING IN THE TREATMENT OF
ADDICTIVE DISORDERS. HE SERVED AS THE FIRST
CHIEF OF COMMUNITY PSYCHIATRY AT HARLEM HOSPITAL.

New York City psychiatrist Lonnie MacDonald, M.D., my friend of more than thirty years, has generously offered his professional expertise and personal experience in two of my previous books. In one of them, Dr. MacDonald used a painting, which hangs in his office, to illustrate the concept of the comfort zone. The title of the painting is *The Circle of Fear* and it is the creation of one of his clients.

The large canvas—perhaps 3 by 4 feet—shows a pretty girl with flowing hair, kneeling in the center of a circle. Inside the circle, there is a calm, light blue sky, and the girl is holding a single flower; she is peaceful and serene. There are words, such as *good* and *yes,* clipped from newspapers and magazines and pasted within the circle as well.

A black and threatening background fills the rest of the large canvas and surrounds the circle. The background is filled with monsters and dragons with knives and swords, and the words *no, don't,* and *bad.*

Depicted through these very dramatic images is a powerful message: If you step over the line, beyond your comfort zone, outside your "circle of fear," you will experience an intense level of anxiety. "Then," according to Dr. MacDonald, "the individual will have two choices: The person can absorb, experience, and deal with the anxious feelings, and thereby enlarge the circle, or the person can be so consumed with fear and anxiety, he or she will retreat to the safer place and jump back inside the circle."

Dr. MacDonald continues, "When the individual has gained sufficient courage to step beyond the limiting perimeter—to make dramatic change—this is the time when encouraging the person to persist is so crucial. Allies are essential because the undertow, the pull, the force to go back, to retreat, is so powerful."

It's easy to see how our comfort zone or circle of fear operates if you are called upon to give a speech in front of five thousand people, climb a fifty-foot ladder, or cook dinner for thirty guests. Those things, for most of us, necessitate stepping outside of our comfort zone and outside our circle of fear and will stir up plenty of uncomfortable feelings.

Yet, some people grew up in such negative circumstances that stress and unhappiness have become their comfort zone. If so, good, happy, and pleasurable feelings can create so much anxiety that people sabotage their positive feelings and jump back into their comfort zone of unhappiness, struggle, negativity, and stress.

Comfort Zones

Dr. Pierre Mornell echoes Dr. MacDonald's thinking.

Pierre Mornell, M.D.

IS A NATIONALLY KNOWN PSYCHIATRIST IN
SAN FRANCISCO'S BAY AREA AND A CONSULTANT ON HIRING
FOR FORTUNE 500 COMPANIES. HE IS THE AUTHOR OF FIVE BOOKS
INCLUDING *GAMES COMPANIES PLAY*, AND *HIRING SMART*.

Dr. Mornell believes that when you step outside your comfort zone, anxious feelings will surface; and, he adds, predictable results will follow.

"Families live within a certain comfort zone. Case in point, let's take a very poor family where both parents are poorly educated. That family structure represents the comfort zone in which the child grows up. Chances are the child will become like his parents or won't stray very far from living in or re-creating that kind of comfort zone. However, suppose instead of failing, that child starts succeeding and graduates from high school. Gradually, he strays from the family comfort zone, and that produces extreme anxiety. People resent others trying to change. Any success, whether it's a graduation, honor, award, the student body presidency, or all A's produces tremendous anxiety or triggers depression, and the child doesn't know why, so it's much easier to simply screw up.

"People yearn to go back to the family. The family may be self-destructive, it may be a terrible and ineffective support system, but it's a support system nonetheless. If a person moves out of his comfort zone he's without the protection of the family and in unknown territory. It's uncomfortable. People are rife with stress, depression, and discomfort until they acquire a new, more flexible set of defenses and strategies to deal with the world as they're learning to navigate through life. Unfortunately, people must invent as they go.

"My wife works with a lot of inner-city children. She has a teenager working for her. It is very threatening for him not to repeat behavior that keeps him wed to his environment. If he does stray, people in his circle may say to him, 'You think you're better than us,' or 'What are you doing with a nine-to-five job and a paycheck?'

"Another low-income adolescent got scholarships to a private high school and to Stanford University. She completed three-and-a-half years at Stanford and was prepared to graduate but didn't. There was too much anxiety associated with graduating, so she dropped out one month before graduation. A year later, after talking with my wife at some length, she returned to college and eventually did graduate.

"I've seen lots of people who were very well educated—Harvard lawyers and CEOs from the best business schools—who repeat the family pattern. To do otherwise provokes too much stress, discomfort, and depression. Repeatedly, people said they wanted to change but couldn't. They had the insight and the intellectual firepower to change, yet never did."

Dr. Mornell concludes his comments about comfort zones with three important ideas: why we change, why we don't change, and why change is so difficult.

"Often, it takes crisis to motivate people to change. There's a tremendous undertow that pulls people back to their comfort zone. A lot of people have painful experiences over and over, yet still don't move out of their comfort zone because it's familiar territory. Being happy, being fulfilled may mean taking a risk. Most people would rather be unhappy than experience that anxiety.

"Pain is a word everybody can understand. It can be a powerful catalyst to cause dramatic change. It has to be severe emotional or physical pain. On a scale of zero to ten, it has to be a twelve."

Meet Maggie, a real estate broker in Portland, Oregon. Her mother was a manic-depressive. Her father was very successful, religiously strict, and very critical. Although she came from an upper middle-class home, Maggie became a sex addict. Addictions know no social boundaries.

Maggie's Compulsion: Sex

"When I was about ten or eleven years old, my father caught me in the basement of our house behind the furnace with a neighborhood boy. He was touching me. It seemed innocent enough. It was just curiosity, mostly his curiosity about me. My dad was very angry, and before sending the boy home, he told us that what we were doing was nasty. The problem was I remained curious, and I actually had sex at age thirteen with a couple of boys in the neighborhood. By high school I was having sex with my boyfriend all the time and flirting with countless other boys. I liked the attention, but I got a bad reputation. It still hurts to this day that I became known in high school as a slut.

"However, it didn't hurt enough that I stopped the behavior. It felt okay to be a bad girl; I was popular. In college I was in a sexual relationship with one guy and also going all the way with a boyfriend-to-be. I hung out with an upper-class crowd and there was plenty of alcohol, drugs, and casual sex.

"I've learned that for most of my adult life I have 'endured' relationships so I wouldn't be alone. When I wasn't in a relationship, I thought one-night stands would help soothe the loneliness. Between relationships—and there were a few along the way—I never really just dated. If I met a guy, and we connected, I always assumed that sex was the next step or even the first step. It never occurred to me to have dinner a few times and gradually introduce sex into a relationship.

"In the past few years, I hooked up with several men in Internet chat rooms and through personal ads. It was not unusual each night for me to be with a complete stranger or sometimes two. I would actually invite these men to my apartment. Then I had a very scary experience involving physical violence, so I stopped looking for sex on the Internet.

"Early last year I received a call from a guy who I had sex with a couple of times. He said he had just tested positive for HIV, and since we had engaged in unprotected sex, he suggested it would be a good idea if I got tested. I did. I had been infected.

"I am now under a doctor's care, and with medication things are okay. I am in an HIV-support group that includes other women with similar stories. The group makes me feel much less alone. We talk openly about our sex lives and that helps, too. What started out as innocent fun certainly didn't end up that way. I had to change. I learned the hard way."

WHY DID I DO THAT?

"My parents, God love them, were pretty messed up. My mother was either on a manic high or in the depths of depression. My father was a religious fanatic. I finally put the pieces together years later in my women's therapy group. I realize that although my mother's condition was a real medical problem, which needed medication and treatment, as a child I saw her as crazy or weak and looking for attention—a victim.

"As a teenager, I grew to hate my father's rules and judgments about my friends and what we did, so I just rebelled. Through sex, I was really looking for attention and love."

MY SUGGESTIONS FOR CHANGE

"I stopped my sex addiction the hard way, and it's been life changing. Hopefully, you don't have to go that route. Maybe you can learn by my mistakes.

"There are support groups and clinics for sex and love addiction. I see them advertised in my local newspapers every week. Find a meeting, sit in the back of the room, and listen. Make a commitment to go to the meetings for a couple of months. If you can relate to what people are talking about, you definitely belong.

"As for casual sex, assume everyone you have sex with is HIV positive. Insist on condoms."

Negative Consequences
Created by Poor Parenting

Children need a lot of time, care, and attention from their parents. Most of all they need love—unconditional with no strings attached. However, parents are human too, and unfortunately many mothers and fathers have personal problems of their own. If parents hurt too much and spend most of their time tending to themselves trying to feel good, it's often at the expense of their children. These troubled parents don't give their children the love their children are entitled to and need. One of these deprived children—and that is not putting it too strongly—may have been you. If messages of security, validation, and support are not internalized during childhood, and if negative messages dominate, children will grow up with a weak sense of self-worth and live in a correspondingly small and unhealthy comfort zone.

Consequently, your comfort zone will probably encompass some type or degree of negative behaviors, relationships, and feelings. Perhaps it is smoking, overeating, drinking excessively, taking drugs, gambling, overspending, working too much, or unsafe sex. Maybe it's your emotional life that's not working and you are living with chronic, low-level anxiety and stress. Negative feelings such as fear, anger, envy, or jealousy may be running your life.

If as a child you did not receive love, then as an adult you still may be trying to get your love, attention, and sense of importance by being very good, helpful, funny, sexy, responsible, smart, sick, bad, or sad.

Lacking confidence, experiencing life as struggle, creating chaos, being unable to trust, and feeling "less than," damaged adults seek "other esteem" to feel good about themselves.

Emotionally neglected or abused people will often pursue others who will tell them they are good, lovable, capable, worthwhile, and important. The search to get this approval will surface in intimate relationships, with close friends, in work situations, and even in leisure activities.

These adults expend incredible energy and valuable time overperforming—attempting to control, manipulate, or sacrifice in order to achieve feelings of wholeness, security, and worth. Their need for affirmation is so great that these people not only look for validation externally in their relationships but also in work or material possessions. However, the sense of "OK-ness," which comes from the outside world, will always be fleeting, and, soon again, insecure and low self-worth people will feel empty, angry, guilty, fearful, and alone again.

To underscore the previous point, a child raised in a troubled home is a relationship wreck and addiction magnet waiting to happen. Without intervention, unhappy children grow up to be unhappy adults. Instead of entering into a positive relationship where partners are validated, needs are met, and love is shared, the insecure adult will seek and/or attract partners who are equally emotionally immature or damaged. The statement made in this type of relationship is not, "I choose to be with you," but "I neeeeeeeeeeeeeeeed you."

If you need someone else to confirm your sense of low self-worth, which is actually what's happening, by criticizing you or acting in such a way that you feel neglected, abandoned, or abused, you'll find someone to do it, so you can blame that other person and not look deeply into yourself for the true cause of your unhappiness. If there is no one else to do it, then you've got to do it yourself. Believe it or not, your own punishing self-talk and actions can be as harmful as anything that may come from another person. For these individuals, their often dependent and destructive primary relationships are a mirror of their past, produce pain and suffering, and will ultimately fail.

Comfort Zones and Self-Worth Inventory

Being successful, happy, and fulfilled are unfortunately outside the comfort zone for too many people. In the face of low self-worth and in reaction to anxiety, they must retreat into their comfort zone of unhappiness, stress, and struggle. Once you become self-destructive and you're used to it, you may feel more comfortable with harmful behavior than healthy behavior. That's often why people abuse themselves physically, mentally, or emotionally.

Business owners take an inventory from time to time. On a personal level it's a good idea as well. The journey of life is inward, not upward, so in order to get a handle on who you are and how you feel about yourself, begin by filling out this inventory focused on your self-esteem and your day-to-day comfort zone.

Self-esteem plays *the* pivotal role in creating your comfort zone. Your positive and negative thoughts and feelings about yourself determine how you live.

Spontaneously respond yes or no to these statements.

I am lovable.	❏ Yes	❏ No
Others are lucky to have me as a friend.	❏ Yes	❏ No
I am an interesting person.	❏ Yes	❏ No

I am fun company.	❏ Yes	❏ No
My primary relationship(s) is (are) fairly effortless.	❏ Yes	❏ No
I take care of my health, eat and sleep well, and exercise.	❏ Yes	❏ No
I am good at my job and enjoy going to work each day.	❏ Yes	❏ No
Most of my needs are being met.	❏ Yes	❏ No
I am happy.	❏ Yes	❏ No
I am a good person.	❏ Yes	❏ No

Your comfort zone and self-worth go hand in hand. If a constant barrage of negative messages was the legacy of your childhood, those messages form the basis of your comfort zone and may be running your life today. If you respond no to any of the above questions, you may either be judging yourself too harshly and self-acceptance may be in order, or positive actions may produce more desirable self-esteem.

One way to enhance self-esteem is to avoid self-destructive behaviors and relationships, which leave you feeling bad, sad, angry, "less than," or guilty.

Give some thought to these questions.

What are three behaviors you do regularly that leave you feeling mad, depressed, deflated, or guilty?

_____

_____

_____

Are there any personal or professional relationships that cause you to feel angry, discounted, marginalized, ignored, or put down? _____

_____

_____

_____

_____

Write down three negative messages you received when you were a child—directly or indirectly, overtly or covertly, by action or inaction, through behavior or speech.

_____

_____

_____

List three overall feelings that seem to motivate your daily life.

_____

_____

_____

To enhance your self-esteem and enlarge your comfort zone, take a risk and do estimable things.

What do you do better than just about anyone else you know?

_____

_____

_____

_____

Do it.

What are you afraid of doing that you really want to do?

_____

_____

_____

_____

Do it.

What do you love to do that makes you happy?

_____

_____

_____

_____

Do it.

CHAPTER FOUR

SELF-DEFEATING BEHAVIORS

When do habits cross the line and move into the arena of addictions, obsessions, and compulsions?

What is the definition of a habit?

What's the difference between a habit and an addiction?

How do you define a compulsion?

What's an obsession?

Whenever I do research for a book, I begin by going to the dictionary. Here's what I discovered in Webster's.

Habit: *(a) A behavior pattern acquired by frequent repetition or physiologic exposure that shows itself in regularity or increased facility of performance. (b) An acquired mode of behavior that has become nearly or completely involuntary.*

Addiction: *(a) Compulsive use of habit-forming drugs. (b) To surrender to do or devote (oneself) to something habitually or obsessively.*

Compulsion: *An irresistible impulse to perform an irrational act.*

Obsession: *Persistent disturbing preoccupation with an often-unreasonable idea or feeling.*

Psychiatrist Pierre Mornell explains the range of human behavior and clarifies what's normal and what's not.

"With all behaviors, there's a spectrum of 10 percent that is very self-defeating and self-destructive, and may lead a person into a hospital, the gutter, or jail. Another 10 percent of our behavior produces no dramatic effect at all. There's probably a bell-shaped curve in between.

"At one end of the curve are rituals that are within the range of so-called normal behaviors. We have a cup of coffee in the morning, go to the gym, or walk the dog. Habits might include a salad at lunch, driving to work on the same route at the same time every day, or going to bed at midnight. We all have rituals that are within the range of so-called normal.

"There are addictive behaviors to alcohol, cigarettes, food, and drugs. Then there are obsessive-compulsive behaviors and phobias. (We live near the Golden Gate Bridge; some people are terrified to go near it.) There are many sexual perversions; abusive relationships in which women have a pattern of marrying men who beat them; people who are very competetive have to win even if it means cheating; and those who compulsively work eighteen hours a day—they never stop.

"Those are some examples that I think are arrayed along a spectrum of human behavior. One hundred years from now, medical and psychiatric professionals will take note of our rather naive understanding of behavior and they will, no doubt, discover not only medications to treat addictions more successfully than they do now, but will discover a lot more about the why, the *dynamics* of it all."

An addiction is a behavior you want to stop but can't. Some have a chemical component, some don't. My father was an alcoholic and growing up in an alcoholic home was not fun. I made a vow that I was never going to be like my father who was often loud and emotionally abusive, drove under the influence frequently, and at times was a falling-down alcoholic. But despite my intentions, I became an alcoholic too. Like father, like son? Environment or genetics?

Genetics Revisited

Dr. Dean Hamer of the National Cancer Institute tackles the environment/genetics debate. He believes that *all* addictive behaviors have a substantial genetic component.

"Most people take pleasure out of whatever activities release dopamine—the brain's feeling-good chemical—and are satisfied. Other people engage in addictive behaviors because they are genetically predisposed to repeat any stimulus that gives them that sort of pleasure. They are the ones who are more likely to keep on drinking, taking cocaine, or seeking sex, even when it has lost its pleasurable effect. What's interesting is that, as you repeat these activities and release more and more dopamine into the brain, the brain adjusts and the cells that normally receive the dopamine signal actually begin to wither and die off. As a result, when the person doesn't have the stimulus, when they don't have a drink or some coke going up their nose, their brain feels bad or improperly stimulated. Their dopamine-sensing apparatus has essentially gotten used up. Seeking to make the brain feel good is what makes people engage in addictive behaviors.

"Eating is an interesting behavior because it has such strong biological and genetic components. The same gene that lets some people burn off fat more rapidly than others is also involved in hunger.

"People who burn fat more slowly are hungrier. Serotonin, the chemical that's involved in depression and anxiety, is also involved in hunger and overeating. So, eating a chocolate bar is like instant Prozac. The candy bar changes serotonin levels so that the brain doesn't feel so bad. It's a quick fix. But in today's world, people judge themselves on how they appear; so, given that fact, the short-term relief from eating the chocolate bar is probably offset somewhat more by the negative impact it has upon a person's self-esteem."

Meet Sue, an attorney in the District of Columbia, who's struggled with a food addiction.

Sue's Compulsion: Overeating

"I have always been overweight. For the first forty-five years of my life, I believed it was okay, and I believed that I was satisfied.

"I was satisfied emotionally because my daddy—one of the absolutely most important persons in my life—said that I was beautiful and that I was smart. I was satisfied culturally because I was the big-breasted black woman with the ample backside, and I was viewed as sturdy. I was satisfied socially because I performed well in my many jobs and I was active in schools and church and people sought me out. I was satisfied professionally because I was assisting the director of a government agency. I was satisfied physically because I loved to eat.

"Then, one Saturday morning a few years ago, when I was about to get out of bed, a pain shot through my right leg with such force that I bolted upright and screamed. I thought it was just a cramp, but it wouldn't stop and I just kept screaming and crying. I dragged myself out of bed and started massaging the right side of my body from upper hip to lower calf. Eventually, I was able to walk, with difficulty. I endured a painful Sunday, and on Monday, I went to see my doctor.

"My doctor, who normally was very chatty, quietly examined me while I talked a mile a second about what must have been wrong with me: a previous injury, a weird sleeping position, or something else. At the end of her examination, she announced her diagnosis: 'You're fat.' I was shaken. I said, 'I may be a little heavy, but I don't think . . .' She quickly cut me off and restated, 'You're fat.' I angrily said, 'You don't have to be so mean and. . . .' She enunciated, 'You are fat; you weigh almost 275 pounds.' Now she had my attention.

"I had no idea that, at five feet almost four inches, I weighed as much as 275 pounds. I simply could not believe it. My doctor looked me in the eyes and said, 'Are you ready? Are you ready?' She was asking me if I was ready to do something about this weight. In hindsight, she was really asking me if I was ready to tackle my real problem: self-control.

"I now began to realize that I had never really denied myself anything that I ever wanted. I either bought, earned, or was given what I wanted. This was the way it was with food: I ate whatever and whenever I wanted. I even allowed myself to think that it wasn't a bad thing. I was wrong. I was killing myself.

"I also became aware that I really wasn't as satisfied, emotionally, culturally, professionally, and socially, as I had believed. How could I have been? I was not healthy.

"Yet, I also knew that I did not want to go on a diet—and I told my doctor so! Whereupon my doctor informed me that I would not be placed on a diet: 'That's temporary,' she said. She continued that I would undergo a complete eating adjustment plan—a plan for life. She said that I would be able to eat and drink anything that I desired, so long as I exercised control and moderation. She told me that I would find personal freedom within these limitations.

"I was already a member of a gym, and so I began attending extra classes. I planned my meals to include more veggies and fewer starches. Needless to say, after some really rough starts, crying buckets of tears, a shot of B12, and extremely sore muscles, I saw results. I liked what I was doing and I became interested in spinning classes, which is indoor cycling on stationary bicycles. Under the tutelage of a fabulous instructor, I was able to complete two AIDS Rides from Durham, North Carolina, to Washington, D.C., about 340 miles.

"More importantly, because I was moderating my eating, I began to personally control myself in other areas of my life as well. I discovered patience and, with that, less tension. Certain people and particular situations no longer vexed me, or at least didn't vex me as much. Along with exercise, prayer became more of an integral part of my daily routine.

"I still have a way to go and I am really working at whittling away these pounds. I know what I have to do. It will take time and I can handle it. For me, life outside my new boundaries is unmanageable; life within my new boundaries is living."

No one gets up in the morning and says, "I think I'll get addicted to food, sex, cocaine, work, the Internet, pornography, or alcohol."

I have a picture of myself, which was probably taken when I was six or seven years old. It's one of those two- by three-inch prints taken at elementary school. Every kid would order a ton of them, give them out to family, relatives, and friends, and still have a batch left over. When I look at the picture objectively, I see in that child's eyes hurt, anger, a kind of defiance, and loneliness. You can tell this kid is in for some real trouble.

Like one of my heroes, movie actor James Dean, I was a teenage rebel without a cause. Dean only made three movies before he died in a car crash. In his last role in *Giant*, Dean played a rags to riches oil baron, Jett Rink, who, at a black-tie celebration dinner that should have been the high point of his life, delivers a grandiose, pathetic, and drunken speech. That scene resonates for me with some horror as I remember my father's frequent behavior at the dinner table, and my own drunk and senseless ramblings on a number of occasions. (Both Dean and Rink are classic examples of self-defeating behavior at its worst when they both had reached the pinnacle of their professions.)

An alcoholic cannot predict with *certainty* (very important word choice) the number of drinks he or she will have, the amount of time that will be spent drinking, or their behavior once they start drinking. That's it. That was me.

This is not a book about alcoholism. The literature of recovery says that alcohol abuse is a symptom. As I wrote earlier, sober up a drunken thief and you still have a thief. So it was. So I was. For years after I quit drinking and abusing prescription drugs, I used cigarettes, people, work, and money to re-create the stresses, struggles, failures, and disappointments of my childhood and teenage years.

The powerful influences of childhood cannot be discounted or denied; however, the same parental influences can affect two children in the same family differently.

Dr. Nathaniel Branden addresses this psychological mystery.

Nathaniel Branden, Ph.D.

IS THE AUTHOR OF TWENTY BOOKS INCLUDING

THE BESTSELLING *THE SIX PILLARS OF SELF-ESTEEM,*

THE PSYCHOLOGY OF SELF-ESTEEM, AND *HONORING THE SELF.*

IN ADDITION TO HIS PRIVATE PSYCHOTHERAPY PRACTICE,

HE CONSULTS WITH BUSINESS ORGANIZATIONS ON THE USE

OF SELF-ESTEEM PRINCIPLES IN THE WORKPLACE.

"Let me tell you a story. A child, being incredibly impressionable, watches his parents struggle, argue, and scrape by with their finances. However, you never know what conclusions the child will draw from what he's seeing. One who sees this might grow up and be very conscientious, scrupulous, and thoughtful about money in a very sane, balanced way—not wanting to be at all like the parent who was so irresponsible when the child was young. Another child in the same family feels, unconsciously to be sure, 'Well, if I'm like my father, he'll have to love me.' The desire for the father's love or approval leads unconsciously to emulating some of the father's (irresponsible) behavior."

Dr. Branden offers another example.

"There are twin brothers. One is an alcoholic and the other is a teetotaler. Naturally, this captures the interest of a psychologist. So, the psychologist goes to the alcoholic and says, 'You know, you're a pretty heavy drinker. Do you have any opinion of how you developed this habit?' The alcoholic answers, 'That's pretty easy to explain. That's no mystery at all. My father was an alcoholic, so you could say I learned to drink at my father's knee.' The psychologist writes this down and goes to visit the second brother. He asks a similar question, and the teetotaler laughs and says, 'My God, there's no mystery at all. It's very easy to explain. You see, my father was an alcoholic. I learned at his knee that alcohol is poison so I choose not to drink.'

"Many people observe that most alcoholics come from alcoholic families, but they don't add that most people who come from alcoholic families don't become alcoholics. You've got to look at both sets of facts. It isn't the case that one is true and the other is false, but rather one is true for some people and one is true for others.

"People often look for simple explanations to explain behavior. For example, they may believe that a significant or extreme past event is the cause of a specific behavior today. The truth is we really don't know what a person will infer from any event. It's not only what happened; it's the meaning a person attaches to what's happened that's important. The moral of these stories is that between the original event and a person's later behavior, the great mysterious variable is the interpretation the individual puts on whatever happened and that's often quite unpredictable."

Whatever the addiction—debt, work, sex, cigarettes, alcohol, drugs, etc.—keep in mind: It's not about the symptom.

Addictions make you feel good when you don't, and they dull emotional, mental, and physical pain when you want and need it to be dulled. Denial makes the continuation of the behavior legitimate in your own eyes. Addictions also block out reality, so, you do wake up one morning (or ten years later) and realize that you are living in a pile of problems, and have fallen into a mental, emotional, financial, physical, and spiritual hole. Those miserable and very real circumstances are compounded by the fact that you cannot quit doing what you are doing.

Meet Sam, a building contractor in Providence, Rhode Island, who's struggled with alcohol.

Sam's Compulsion: Alcohol

"I grew up in a household rife with alcoholism, drug addiction, mental illness, and violence. As a kid, if I needed anything—support, guidance, stability, and love—I assumed that the adults in my life were so preoccupied with getting away from one difficult situation or the next that they would never give me what I needed, so I simply never asked.

"By fifteen, I drank every day, all day. Even so, somehow I managed to graduate from high school and get admitted to college. However, before the high school graduation ceremony, I got so drunk that after I was handed my diploma in front of several thousand people, I couldn't remember whether to go down the stairs on the left or right side of the stage. Simple task, but I was really lost.

"I drank for another twelve years and I found myself in that bewildered state many times—the spot where most sane or rational people would know which way to go or at least have the sense to ask someone for guidance or direction. My only solution was to have another drink. Once I started, I couldn't stop, and never really wanted to stop. Even when faced with endless pain, loss, and failure at how to do anything but drink, I experienced tremendous relief from drinking as I muddled through life.

"By day, I held a prestigious position with the state legislature and by night I usually drank alone in a drafty, dark, and sparsely furnished apartment. It didn't add up. At some point, it finally dawned on me that perhaps my drinking and, by then, drugs, were really obstacles. The 'now what?' question finally had an answer, and I knew that there were places to go for help. For the first time, I started to believe I could live without drinking.

"When I was ready, help was literally around the corner. On the last night of a week-long binge, I was quite slammed and then got hit with the usual depression, worry, anxiety, and, once again, not knowing what I did the previous night. At that moment, I picked up the phone and called an alcohol treatment center. On the phone I babbled because of drunkenness, cried because of weariness, and resisted because I was scared. The intake nurse listened and finally asked—and I honestly think this is the first time someone had done so—if I *wanted* help to stop drinking. I said yes. The treatment center, visible from my apartment window, was only two blocks away! At twenty-eight, I checked in and began to clean up the mess my life had become.

"I no longer doubted whether I was an alcoholic. In my gut I knew, and I knew I was in trouble. There I discovered that I had the disease of alcoholism and left untreated it would eventually make my life worse or certainly kill me. What I needed to do became clearer. After leaving treatment, I became a committed member of 12-Step programs and I still do not drink.

"The first step I took was to change the people in my life. Sure they drank too and moderately, but they also had successful lives. Eventually, I started to have higher expectations for myself. The possibility of success started to emerge on many fronts. The chaos, running from conflict, failing in relationships or jobs because they were hard seemed less of an option.

"Somehow I had managed to build a career and surround myself with people who expected me to show up and stay around. These people showed some concern for me beyond what I had done or did, but had appreciation for who I was.

"In the end, I had to face the fact that I was not a very successful drinker. More evidence was unnecessary. Eventually, however,

I became a successful sober person. I kept those caring people in my life and found yet more support from others in recovery. Having other people to help me has been so very important. I picked up many new skills, life got better, and the real work began. That was more than seventeen years ago I'm proud, happy, and relieved to say.

"People around me continue to drink—colleagues, friends, and family—and do so sanely and manage to make their lives work. My drinking was anything but sane, it was irrational. My life was screwed up because I drank, and I drank because my life was screwed up. Recently a newspaper article reported some progress among scientists in finding a pill that would cure alcoholism. I'm not sure about others, but if given a choice, I don't think I would take it. Letting go of alcohol has given me a lot: greater patience with myself and others, and a profound level of self-awareness and self-acceptance that has subsumed the hopelessness, fear, and befuddlement of my drinking life."

WHY DID I KEEP DOING THAT?

"I now understand that alcoholism is a disease. With a long line of alcoholism on both sides of the family, I have a genetic predisposition to drink to excess. Living with people who were entirely focused on managing their own difficulties made it impossible for me to be heard or acknowledged much by the adults in my life. That created a pattern of isolation and feeling of loneliness that seemed normal. In retrospect, drinking was probably the safest thing for me to do. When I was drunk, life didn't seem so bad.

"As a young man it also seemed the logical thing to do—everyone else was doing it and the payoff was the attention and companionship of others. Honestly, it felt good—at first, and even at the end—though I didn't see the connection between the difficulties I was having in my life (relationships, jobs, health, depression) and drinking.

"There is nothing rational about repeatedly drinking to the point of throwing up, losing control, and blacking out. I had grown weary of feeling so awful about myself because of my inability to lead a 'normal' and functional life, such as showing up at work. Only after stopping did I make the connection."

MY SUGGESTION FOR CHANGE

"If someone came to me today with an alcohol and/or drug problem and asked for my advice, these would be my suggestions.

"Staying stopped is not something people can do alone. At least I couldn't. Alcoholism is very isolating and most active alcoholics by choice or circumstance live in worlds that get smaller and smaller as we sicken. There is little, if any, accountability if we spend all of our time alone or with people who approve, enable, or do not openly disapprove of drinking and the resulting behavior.

"Alcoholics who hope to get better need to enlarge their world. I began to watch how others managed life day-to-day. 12-Step programs have worked for me. Therapy worked. I moved to a less marginal neighborhood. I left a job where drinking was an important part of the culture. I reacquainted myself with old friends. In doing so, I discovered that many people who I had not seen in years were, in fact, sober. I joined a gym. I had my first physical as an adult. I had a dental check-up. In other words, I began to do what everyone else does. For me these actions were extraordinary. For everyone else they are normal. I am not normal. I am an alcoholic and make a decision each day to not drink and live a sober life."

Alcohol, drugs, cigarettes, and food are a few of the more obvious addiction substances. These all have a chemical component. But all addictive behaviors are not necessarily physically related. People also get addicted to the Internet, shopping, work, or sex.

While it's easier to see the pain, loneliness, and self-destruction of a drug addict, alcoholic, or compulsive gambler (usually overt behaviors), other self-defeating compulsions—far less dramatic and noticeable—can be just as insidious.

While it is true, as Dr. Branden noted, that siblings coming out of the same dysfunctional home may indeed interpret the experience differently, there seems little disagreement among most mental health professionals that everyone who comes out of a troubled home pays a price.

Meet John, a midlevel financial analyst at one of New York City's most prestigious consulting firms, who's struggled with putting things off.

John's Compulsion: Procrastination

"I have a reoccurring problem that has plagued me for most of my adult life. I leave things until the last minute and then rush to complete them. I'm not exactly sure how the problem started, but it has affected me personally and professionally. I've missed college and graduate school assignment deadlines that have affected not only my grades, but also those of my peers when we worked on group projects. In graduate school, I had trouble finding people to work with because I had a reputation for waiting until the last minute and producing shoddy work or no work at all. Some of my classmates swore never to work with me and they didn't.

"At work, I've experienced the exact same problem—I've missed deadlines for projects or started work on things so late that I've delivered garbage to my clients. In one job, I never moved up and was shunned on new projects because I under-delivered on so many occasions that people didn't want to work with me. In another job, there were days when I didn't do any work at all. In one example, I had a case study that was due on a Friday. It was really due the previous Friday, but I had come up with some excuse as to why I couldn't produce it on the original schedule. Finally, the due date appeared and I called in sick. Over the weekend, it gnawed at me, but I didn't do anything about it. On the following Monday, my boss had to write the case study himself. It was terrible.

"I'm not sure what it is that drives me to repeat this behavior over and over again, but it is not healthy. My self-esteem is horrible as a result of years of cumulative near-failure. What is it that drives me to under perform? What can I do to break this pattern of self-defeating behavior?

"I have chosen today to work to develop habits that reinforce the 'good' behavior. Instead of shrinking into my shell, I reach out to my teammates and ask for their help. This is an important step for me, reaching out to others. It's not something I do well. In my need to please, I have learned to smile and pretend that I'm not overworked, that I can do anything and everything that's being asked of me. I need to unlearn this behavior. I also have to start behaving like an adult, not just wanting to be liked by everyone. This is often difficult for me, because I want others' approval so badly.

"In personal relationships, I've also experienced similar problems with procrastination. I haven't acted when I should have and some very special people have slipped away from me. I've also gotten myself into and maintained some stupid relationships simply because I was too lazy to work at it harder or demand more. After a particularly disappointing and unchallenging relationship, I swore off relationships entirely until I figured out it was a need for approval and low expectations that were driving me to operate below my potential.

"In a matter of months, without even looking for it, I found myself attracted to a very challenging woman, someone who I had to work hard to impress and who demanded high standards of me. I rose to the challenge, enjoying myself as I did so, and now find myself happily married to that woman.

"Where have I found the strength to look at this deep insecurity of mine? I have found it in my relationship with my wife. It gives me great strength that she is accepting of my flaws and that she loves me even when I feel unlovable. I feel that she will always be there for me and this is a great strength to me.

"I'm in a new job now and find that I am developing a good reputation. People want to work with me. They seek me out when they have free time. I'm known as a team player and a major contributor."

Why Did I Keep Doing That?

"Looking back on my behavior, I can see a couple of things that probably led to the initial behaviors associated with my growing habit of procrastination.

"As an Army brat, I moved around a lot as a child. Like many 'global nomads,' I had some truly wonderful experiences, but I also learned some bad habits that I am always in the process of unlearning. One of the things that I learned early on was that since I was always moving every couple of years, I could wait problems out and they would simply go away when I moved! At least this is what I thought at first. I also learned that it was too painful to keep investing in deep and strong relationships that I couldn't keep as I moved around the world. Finally, I developed some deep insecurities associated with always feeling like an outsider, even here at 'home,' and always having to reestablish myself in new schools and communities. All of these things are common attributes of people who move around a lot and live outside of their native culture."

MY SUGGESTIONS FOR CHANGE

"What would I suggest to someone with a similar problem?

"My success in overcoming this problem—an ongoing and never-ending struggle—has been first to recognize my background and the habits that I've developed as a result of it, and then develop new habits of addressing things in full when they come my way.

"Communicating, or 'managing expectations,' has also been important in my success—I've found that my family and workmates are much more flexible and understanding when I share my plans to complete a particular project or assignment, and negotiate expectations, timelines, and projected outcomes. Key to all of this is my own desire to do better, be more successful, and get out of a cycle of negative feedback and low expectations. Family and friends have been critical in this success. Meeting regularly with a men's group, led by a professional psychologist, has also helped me learn how to develop the strong interpersonal bonds that are required for success in overcoming procrastination. Some people prefer one-on-one sessions with a professional—for me, since my problem was in creating lasting relationships and following through on commitments, I've found the group environment to be very helpful."

I often meet people who are in jobs they really dislike or actually hate. They got into their career early on, started to climb a work ladder, moved up a few notches, made some money, got some raises, married, and/or took on major financial obligations that required them to keep going, whether they liked it or not. They find themselves at midlife locked in and regretting the other road not traveled. While some people use money issues to cause themselves pain, others may do it with a job or career.

Parental Expectations

Some people use their jobs or careers as mega-destructive behavior to make themselves unhappy and stay inside their (very undesirable) comfort zone of negative feelings. For insight into why people do this, I talked with human behavior specialist Marylin Dyer Blair.

Marylin Dyer Blair, M.A.

IS A CAREER AND JOB COUNSELOR, AND OWNER,
PARTNER, AND PRESIDENT OF THE MARYLAND CONSULTING GROUP.
SHE HOLDS A MASTER'S DEGREE IN HUMAN BEHAVIOR,
IS A CERTIFIED MANAGEMENT CONSULTANT, AND HAS MORE
THAN TWENTY YEARS EXPERIENCE IN ORGANIZATION
DESIGN AND DEVELOPMENT.

Marylin Dyer Blair explains:

"I encounter a fair number of people in their thirties, forties and fifties who struggle because they entered a job, field, or discipline just by chance or because it was an expectation of their parents. One day they woke up and said, 'I'm worn out.' While it's true that some of them just bounced into where they are, a lot of it starts with parental expectations—following in Dad or Mom's footsteps. Dad or Mom may not even say it. It may be implied or inferred. For instance, it is often expected that one or more of the children will go into the family business even though the child may not be suited for it.

"People may keep getting mired in the wrong job or career, work for unreasonable bosses, or make many mistakes in their work. They may even ask themselves, 'Why do I keep doing that?' They probably need help; however, most people go to their friends instead of a professional. Sometimes, those friends are in the same boat as they are, so it winds up being a gripe session. They both air their mistakes and complaints, and take great delight in doing so. They complain and complain, and go on and on. People do this for years. It becomes a chronic condition, a chronic lifestyle."

An older teenager with a serious dislike for academics once asked me, "What should I do?" after he had unsuccessfully and unceremoniously left his third or fourth college. I asked him a few questions, including what was the most fun he'd ever had. He responded with no hesitation, "Sports." So, I asked, "If you could do anything you wanted to do—have any job you wanted—what would it be?" He responded, "I'd be a golf pro." I said, "Why don't you give it a try?" I remember his response to this day. I can still hear it. It came after a long pause in the conversation. He said, "What would they say?" *They* turned out to be his father, mother, and brother.

Marylin Dyer Blair observes:

"There's a lot of fuzzy thinking about what I expect of myself, what you expect of me, what my friends expect of me, what acquaintances expect of me. Many of us develop patterns of behaving that, while they may make us unhappy, we will repeat over and over because we never examined these expectations and unearthed what's causing us to do what we do. Once expectations are examined carefully and resolved, people who are struggling can make exciting changes."

Our young friend packed his bags a few weeks later and moved to Florida. After working at a few golf courses, he earned his PGA Class A card and became an assistant teaching pro. While he no longer works in golf, he uses his golfing skills and personality very successfully in business today. He hits the ball a mile and I would take him for a partner any day, no questions asked.

Wrong Jobs and Wrong Careers

Ms. Dyer Blair reveals how people can tell if they are in the right or wrong job or career, and thus identify if it is their work that is making them unhappy:

"Work, especially for men and increasingly now for women, is how we define ourselves to a large degree. If you go to a party, one of the first questions people ask is 'What do you do?' It's become a standard. Sometimes, when people are phasing out of one career into another, changing jobs, or looking for one, 'What do you do?' is one of the toughest questions they face because they don't have a ready answer. It's as if the monogram has been ripped off their shirt—it's a loss of identity.

"People get into the wrong jobs and the wrong careers. One of the challenges parents have is to guide children, not direct them, as they set out to find work for themselves. Let me give you an example.

"A client of mine has a very bright daughter. She had finished a degree in mathematics and entered a very prestigious architectural school. She started having sleep interruptions and she didn't like the classes she was taking. Her father asked me to talk with her because she was so unhappy. I had her send me her college transcripts. When we sat down to talk, she said 'I hate what I'm doing', and I said 'Good for you. It's as important to know what you don't like doing as it is to know what you do like doing. You may have been a math major, but when I reviewed your materials from college, I quickly saw that every elective you took was in psychology. You may want to be a psychologist and not even know it.'

"We had done a style profile and she was clearly a people person. She was extremely bright, so she could handle the grind of math and architecture, but it wasn't fulfilling for her. The end of the story is that she got her degree in industrial psychology and the last I heard she was very happy.

"She started a math degree because her dad is a math wizard and she admires him. They have a very close relationship. As she got into math, though, she realized it really wasn't who she was and it didn't help define her as a person. So, she started experiencing sleep problems. Most of us ignore physical symptoms and don't see the connection between what our body is trying to tell us and what's going on in our jobs or careers. I see that a lot."

In the following example, Marylin Dyer Blair describes the executive who was indeed playing in the right game but at the wrong position. In his case, he was trying to live up to a present-day set of expectations. Bad job choices and ill-chosen careers are a symptom of a deeper conflict.

"The president of a corporate division was in charge of a start-up operation, but he didn't like making quick decisions. This man is a very sharp individual and never had any bumps in his career. He'd always been very successful. His boss created very strenuous situations to challenge him and give him the kind of opportunity he had told his boss he wanted. He had gotten into a groove of proving himself over and over and over again. He saw himself as a problem solver, which he was, but his style didn't fit a start-up operation. It fit a more mature organization. The bottom line was he was trying to meet his own expectations and those of his boss.

"We had many talks and I encouraged him to look for a position where he could use his financial background, which was heavily oriented to sifting through information and making multiple decisions but taking a considerable amount of time to do it. He's since taken a wonderful job, which fits his analytic style and financial background, and he's extremely happy."

Marylin Dyer Blair has an important closing thought:

"It's very common that a person who is having problems in his or her personal life may also have problems in the workplace as well, and, of course, vice versa. By identifying the key people in your life—I call them 'milestone people'—you can often cobble together the kind of person you are today and what expectations and influences guide your choices in everything from work to friends to marriage partners. When you were growing up, with whom did you spend the most time? What was that person like? Are you similar to or different from that person? If you want to know the woman or the man, know the child."

Self-Destructive Behavior

Let's pause here and sum up the larger picture of self-destructive behavior. Dr. Steve Pieczenik defines it for us and applies the definition to a variety of situations and finally to himself.

Steve Pieczenik, M.D.

IS THE FIRST PSYCHIATRIST TO HAVE RECEIVED A
DOCTORATE IN INTERNATIONAL RELATIONS. HE HAS OVER
TWENTY YEARS EXPERIENCE RESOLVING INTERNATIONAL CRISES
AND HOSTAGE SITUATIONS FOR THE DEPARTMENT OF STATE
FOR FOUR ADMINISTRATIONS. AS A TELEVISION PRODUCER AND
WRITER, HE IS CO-CREATOR OF THE *NEW YORK TIMES* BESTSELLING
TOM CLANCY'S OP-CENTER AND TOM CLANCY'S
NET FORCE BOOK AND TELEVISION SERIES.

Dr. Pieczenik explains:

"There is a repetitive nature to self-destructive behavior. When we discuss it, we should have a very clear understanding that it is behavior in which an individual, a group, or even a nation engages that is injurious but, nevertheless, garners some type of reward or advantage.

"When I worked in the hospital, we had patients who cut their hands and wrists repeatedly. The question, then, is what advantage does anyone gain by doing something that's injurious to himself? I found out they would do it at times of high stress, when they felt they couldn't handle a particular situation, or they were avoiding a confrontation. Usually it had something to do with intimacy. In many ways, the wrist cutting was a way of controlling their own destiny and feeling very powerful at the same time. So, in their minds, the benefits outweighed the disadvantages of what we would perceive as self-destructiveness.

"We see that very clearly in martyrdom. In certain Muslim sects, the notion of submission to Allah's will can be manipulated by religious individuals with political aspirations. In Palestine, children fight Israeli soldiers. While the parents weep for their children who have died in suicide bombings, they feel they have sacrificed their children for a greater good. So martyrdom becomes the rationalization for the self-destructive behavior. It's exceedingly self-destructive to the Palestinian people, and it's certainly self-destructive to the Israelis because the Palestinians retaliate with suicide attacks and Israelis die too.

"These examples of self-destructiveness are similar to what I see in cases of anorexia, bulimia, alcoholism, and heroin addiction. One of the most devastating addictions I've seen is gambling. I really don't know why it's more difficult to treat than other addictions. Gamblers are willing to lose *everything*—not almost everything. They've lost their families, their homes, and their jobs. Yet, they have to compulsively go back to gambling.

"Self-defeating behavior is also easy to see in public figures. There's the obvious example with former President Bill Clinton. Seducing an intern in the White House is not just a question of inappropriate behavior; it is pathological behavior. It may indicate that Bill Clinton needs to have his sense of self-worth or self-esteem punished for things he feels he has or has not done. Continuously, as an elected official in both Arkansas and Washington, he got into situations that gave the impression he needed to punish himself by humiliation or embarrassment, followed by the need to say words to the effect of, 'I confess my sins and I'm sorry.' He would then revert back into a pattern of remarkable achievement, self-abuse, self-punishment, and contrition.

"However, no president and vice president have been more self-destructive than George W. Bush and Dick Cheney. Alcohol abuse is in both their pasts. Their more recent actions have destroyed American institutions, foreign countries, and international respect for our country. Their unprovoked war in Iraq has placed us in an isolated, hated, and currently defeated position, which may lead to our own economic and moral bankruptcy."

One of the explanations for the compulsion to repeat from our "menu of possibilities" is "parental expectations" as outlined by Marylin Dyer Blair. Dr. Pieczenik examines this at work with the Kennedy legacy.

"The Kennedy family offers a tragedy of Greek proportions with assassinations, accidents, and plane crashes. The father, Joe Kennedy—the immigrant who became a new type of powerful man—decided that he would create a dynasty through his children. That legacy of pressure came to bear on every one of his sons. Eventually, all of the male Kennedy family members damaged themselves or unconsciously hurt themselves so that they didn't have to bear the burden of being the best. That may have occurred unfortunately with John-John, too, when he flew his plane at a time when it wasn't appropriate. Sadly, the Kennedys are a family that display the kind of self-destructive tragedy that's transgenerational."

One morning while I was watching "Meet the Press," I was

floored when General Norman Schwarzkopf answered a Tim Russert question by saying, "Napoleon said you have to be real careful about war; it can be so exciting, you can grow to love it." Dr. Pieczenik believes that if you look at war, you begin to see its addictive qualities and self-destructiveness on a grander scale.

"The issues of self-destructiveness and repetition globally have bothered me for quite awhile. As a deputy assistant secretary of state in four administrations, I have seen terrorism, counterterrorism, and the horrors of Cambodia, Africa, the Balkans, the Middle East, and now Afghanistan and Iraq. I still don't have an answer. Why does man have this need to continuously engage in some form of war against himself in the name of religion, ethnic differences, territorial imperatives, or class status? It may boil down to one reason, which may be too simplistic, but the conclusion I came to believe is that war is addictive."

Dr. Pieczenik now shines the spotlight on himself.

"I clearly can't be sanctimonious about self-destructiveness. We all have our own self-defeating behaviors. There are certain behaviors that I know I should engage in that would facilitate my health, such as running every day for thirty minutes. Now that's not a lot to ask. I could walk outside for an hour three times a week. That's a simple dictum of cardiology. Because I have a family history of cardiac illness and I'm taking medication, I somehow rationalize the medication is substituting for the exercise when I know very well as a doctor that that's not the case. I find forty-three different excuses. I can give you one right now, that it's too cold outside for me to walk for forty-five minutes. If it were over ninety degrees, I would give you the excuse that it's too hot. Within me there is this self-destructive aspect that will say, 'Steve, you know you have this history, and it's not very much to ask for you to get some exercise. You don't have to overdo it.' And yet I say, 'To hell with that, I'm taking my medication and a little more aspirin.' That kind of self-destructiveness appears within me. The benefit is that I can be what I want to be, which is lazy. This is the self-inflicted punishment for having this terrible gene that I did not choose and for the resentment I feel because I'm irredeemably flawed. So why not choose to beat death? Beat the clock. It would certainly give me more control. In other words, instead of death leaving me, I leave it. It sounds morbid and a little perverse, but self-destructiveness has a morbid quality to it. Self-destructive or harmful or self-defeating behavior can be not doing something, such as exercise, in my case.

"I heard on the radio that all I have to do is exercise and eat the proper foods. All I wanted to hear was 'eat the proper foods.' The exercise, I'll do later.

"When Churchill was in his eighties, he was a pallbearer for one of his friends. They asked him if he exercised. He said, 'No, not whatsoever. I don't do it at all. That's why I'm carrying the casket here for my friend who did.' We look for all kinds of reinforcement and rationalization to justify our behavior."

Regardless of the behavior, addictions are all pretty much the same. They "work" for a while. You use (or do it), abuse, and then cross some kind of imaginary line—and, like chasing a big pile of money in the pot of a poker game, you're in—and you can't get out.

I did it with alcohol and pills. I was the classic textbook alcoholic living a life of anger, worry, depression, and self-pity with thoughts of suicide. I lived my life in fear, looking over my shoulder. G. Douglas Talbott, M.D., director of the Ridgeview Institute in Smyrna, Georgia, calls alcoholism "the disease of loneliness." I know what he means. The word "loneliness" cuts right through me to this day. Even though I enjoyed success on television and was constantly surrounded by people, I felt alone.

At peak tolerance, I was a quart-of-Black-&-White-scotch-and-60-milligrams-of-Valium-a-day addict. Thank God, that nightmare ended more than twenty-five years ago. I write these few lines about me to let you know that even the most self-defeating, harmful, and painful behavior can be stopped and stay stopped.

Actions really do speak louder than words: They can help us achieve or sabotage our goals, contribute to or damage our health, promote or negate our happiness.

Do your behaviors make you feel better or worse about yourself? Do your actions make you feel positive, happy, and enthusiastic about living? Do they make you feel joyful? Or do your behaviors and actions diminish your sense of well-being, your self-worth, your happiness?

Behavior Inventory

This behavior inventory may help you identify that single behavior that has moved out of the "bad habit" category and is now running your life with painfully negative results.

1. Have you identified a specific behavior, which is making you unhappy? _____

_____

_____

_____

2. How does it make you feel? _____

_____

_____

_____

3. Is it causing you severe pain? _____

_____

_____

_____

4. How long has this behavior been going on? _____

_____

_____

_____

5. What "rewards" are you getting from this behavior? _____

_____

_____

_____

6. What will be the benefits of getting rid of this behavior?

_____

_____

_____

7. How will overcoming this behavior make you feel? _____

_____

_____

_____

_____

_____

8. What are the barriers getting in the way of your making this change? _____

_____

_____

_____

9. What actions will you take to bring about this change? ____

_____

_____

_____

10. Will you consider making this change your number one priority for the next month? _____

_____

_____

_____

Unless you are a student of human behavior, chances are you are reading this book with the goal of stopping some repeating behavior that is causing you unhappiness. You may know what the problem is; hopefully you are on the road to the solution.

Faith is the belief in the experiences of other people. It's a definition I heard a long time ago, and it's a beginning that works. Other people have lost weight, quit drugs, stopped gambling, left abusive relationships, or stopped being habitually jealous or angry. The world is full of people who have brought about dramatic changes in their lives. They did it—and so can you.

CHAPTER FIVE

PAINFUL FEELINGS

All you have to do is listen. If we actually heard ourselves talking to, with and at each other, or talking to ourselves, we would be flabbergasted to discover the number of people around us who are negative, critical, and judgmental. Many people are stressed, anxious, depressed, helpless, and hopeless. Fear, guilt, jealousy, envy, and shame run the lives of many others. Similar to self-defeating behaviors and harmful relationships, obsessive thinking, and painful feelings can also be evidence of the compulsion to repeat.

Chris, a Florida bookstore owner, admits to being negative and a chronic worrier. I asked her where that came from. She didn't pause. "From my mother," she replied. "My parents got divorced when I was pretty young, but we had a big family and she worried a lot about all of us."

When it comes to optimism/happiness or pessimism/unhappiness, our feelings about ourselves, other people, and the events in our lives—large and small—play a huge role in the quality of our lives.

Martin E. P. Seligman, Ph.D., the author of the book *Learned Optimism,* believes that pessimism is something that is probably learned, so it can also be unlearned. It's a negative habit, he says, which can be changed.

Worry colors the way Chris sees herself—"I'm just not lucky in dating"—and her view of her world—"I don't think my boss likes me." Our self-talk can play a huge role in whether we see the glass as half empty or half full.

Chris's Compulsion: Pessimism

"My father cheated on my mother and he finally left us when I was nine. My world ended the day he left. I actually blamed my mother for his leaving back then, but their relationship had to end or someone was going to physically get hurt.

"Not too surprisingly, as I grew up, I developed a real negative attitude about people and life. I was pretty sarcastic and real good at pushing people away. I trusted no one and I was critical of most everyone. I just saw the worst in everything. People put up with me, but in retrospect, I don't think they liked me at all.

"One day, I saw a psychologist on a television talk show talking about negativity. His name was Dr. Seligman and I wrote down the title of his book they were talking about, *Learned Optimism,* and went out and bought it. I started reading it and I could see myself on practically every page. It was scary. His whole idea was that negativity is learned, and that you can also learn to be positive. He had several ideas about how people learn to be negative. Looking back at my own life, I could see how my mother was beaten down by life long before my father left. She probably was a very depressed person to begin with. I don't know if I inherited some of her chemistry or I just learned how to be so down from her. I remember that Dr. Seligman said that one of the sources for learning to be negative was 'your mother.'

"I began keeping a notebook and wrote down the situations I ran into each day when I said something negative or critical. I wrote down what my feelings were at the time. Dr. Seligman's book had other suggestions that I started to use.

"I asked my best friend to help me break my habit of being so negative. Every time she heard me say something negative, I had to give her a dollar. I won't tell you about the first two weeks, but even at week three, I still had to shell out $36. It cost me a lot of my money, but it helped me to change. In the end, it was a good thing. My new attitude is like the old joke about the child, happily shoveling the manure in the barn, who says, 'I know there's a pony in here someplace.' I try to find out what's good about things nowadays. I fall back sometimes, but for the most part, I do pretty well. I am a learned optimist today. Dr. Seligman would be proud!"

WHY DID I KEEP DOING THAT?

"Somebody once said to me, 'If you're having any fun, please notify your face.' I was a pretty negative camper. I could scope out the worst in just about anything or anybody. I've discovered that fear is at the bottom of my negativity, pessimism, and being so judgmental. Trying to control the actions and moods of others is in the mix too.

"I was raised in a New England, Irish-Catholic family. I was brought up to build walls for self-protection. One of my brothers said once that if anyone in our family had an emotion, they had to go into another room. Of course, when I was growing up the major tenets of the Catholic Church were fear and guilt. Life is tough sometimes for sure, but I think God wants us to be as happy as we can be right here, right now."

MY SUGGESTIONS FOR CHANGE

"My advice? Simple, get a copy of Dr. Martin Seligman's book *Learned Optimism*.

"Being loose, relaxed, having fun, and seeing the best instead of the worst feels a lot less threatening to me now, and being out of control doesn't seem as dangerous. And I'm more trusting now. My friends tell me I'm a lot more fun to be around, and I'm pretty good at seeing the positive side of people and things."

Sometimes feelings can be so painful; we use substances and devise strategies to block them out altogether. Alcohol, legal or illegal drugs, smoking, gambling, eating, and sex all do the job. Busyness and chaos can achieve the same goal. Meet Timothy, who orchestrated his "craziness" toward that end. Timothy, an American who works in Europe part-time, describes his life of crisis and use of chaotic behaviors to hide his feelings.

Timothy's Compulsion: Chaos

"To me, the chaos is very loud, and it drowns out whatever I don't want to feel. Chaos allows me to avoid feeling. And because it's external, I can create the kind of chaos I want to deal with, or not deal with the parts of me that I don't want to feel.

"The biggest single feeling I want to avoid is loneliness. When I am feeling lonely I can create chaos that doesn't make the loneliness feel so strong. Whatever I'm using to create the chaos becomes my drug.

"Two years ago, I was in Europe. The night before I was to fly back to the United States, I verified the balance in my checking account to make sure I had enough money to get from Dulles airport to downtown Washington, D.C., which is a very expensive taxi trip. Incidentally, over the two previous weeks I had lost about $7,000 in the stock market, which, to me, was a significant amount of money. I confirmed that my checking balance was a little over $140. I have to admit though this was only one of many, many times I had been in a financial squeeze.

"The next day, on the layover in New York during my trip home, I thought, *Well, let me check my account balance just to make sure.* I was shocked. I was over $50 overdrawn and had only seventy-nine cents in my pocket! For the next three hours, I had plenty of time to make myself completely miserable.

"I had been going back and forth to Europe for seven years for periods of anywhere between three to five months. Whenever I was in the United States, I was obsessed with always getting back to Europe. Looking back on it now, I was obsessed with Europe because I had free rein there—free rein to have as much of what I wanted when I wanted it. Whether it was staying out all night in clubs, having lots and lots of sex, living cheap and not working, it all added up to having little responsibility. I was out of my American environment, and I really didn't have to be responsible for myself or to anyone.

"However, the obsession and irresponsibility created total unmanageability and complete chaos.

"When I was sitting on the plane, a light went on. I was like the drug addict who finally runs out of chances. After a friend wired $500 into my checking account and the dust had settled, I made the decision to change. I threw up my hands and prayed, 'Okay God, I've had enough of this chaos. I am willing to never go back to Europe until things are different in my life.'

"Within two months of coming home I got a great job making very good money. I stayed on that job for two years and got my finances in order like never before.

"Today my mortgage and monthly expenses are easily covered, I've got $5,000 in my checking account, $14,000 in stocks, and I am paying off my credit card debt as quickly as I can. However, the biggest part of the past two years was that I fundamentally changed the way I live my life—by not having chaos in it. This was no easy feat.

"I've spent these two years working with a very close friend over dinner every Friday night to understand the role that chaos played in my life. To do so required a great deal of honesty, humility, and recognition of my own insanity.

"As it turned out, chaos was a huge factor in all areas of my life. It affected everything—my sex life, my financial life, my personal relationships, the way I spent my days! I never had peace until I got a handle on the chaos.

"Do I have frantic days today? Absolutely. Does the chaos come back? In very, very tiny pieces. Since the bulk of the craziness has disappeared over the last two years, my level of tolerance for it is much lower, and I don't let it continue for hours, days, and weeks. This change has brought about a huge amount of newfound freedom in my life.

"I have always believed that pain is a great motivator for change. For me, and probably for most people, until something causes me enough pain, I continue to do what I do, even if it causes me trouble. Today, when I have that moment of clarity that 'Something is wrong with this picture,' I can step back, discover what it is, and take whatever action I need to change it."

WHY DID I KEEP DOING THAT?

"I think that the chaos originally came from my childhood and continued into my adult life. I don't think that there is just one thing behind the chaos. I didn't grow up feeling that I was loved or a good person worthy of good things, so I've sought out inappropriate things and created chaos in the process. I can even rationalize the chaos, self-righteously believing that I deserve to have some validation—even in inappropriate ways—because I never got it as a kid.

"I created the chaos in my life so I wouldn't feel the feelings of fear, anger, and loneliness. It's a defense mechanism, for sure. I can see that now, but it has been extremely difficult for me to get in touch with that. That moment of clarity on the plane was my beginning."

MY SUGGESTIONS FOR CHANGE

"There is a reason for chaos—going out to a bar every night, waking up late, showing up for work late again, or getting fired. There's a reason for looking at porn or looking at sex on the Internet—or for going on another shopping spree and going over your credit limit and not having enough money to pay the rent.

"If someone came to me with lots of chaos in his life I would tell him or her to *listen*. When a family member, friend, or co-worker questions the way you are living, listen.

"There are therapists in every small town and big city in the country. We live in a time when there is a support program for just about every problem—from alcohol and drugs, to sex and relationships, to overeating and overspending.

"When you finally push the door of willingness open by listening to that family member, good friend, or co-worker, I say pick up the phone and start seeking out the places you can get help. But *listen*. Listen to what people are saying to you."

The late Penelope Russianoff, Ph.D., wrote the brilliant book *When Am I Going to Be Happy?*, subtitled *How to Break the Emotional Bad Habits That Make You Miserable.* Answering her own question, Dr. Russianoff observes:

"What is a negative emotional habit? Like any habit, it is a learned reflex. It is a response that becomes unthinking and automatic through constant repetition. The drug addict is hooked on heroin or some other dangerous substance. But others become guilt addicts, or anxiety addicts, or rejection addicts, or fall into any of a dozen other negative emotional obsessions."

Casting about for why pessimism, negativity, self-loathing, and other emotional bad habits take hold, Dr. Russianoff says: "Obviously formative childhood influences and experiences are crucial."

In her book's section on anger, for example, Dr. Russianoff continues:

"Very many of my patients, I find, have picked up the anger habit by observing a parent. Children who see a parent as frightening and forbidding are apt to copy this behavior. Why? Frankly, because it appears to work for them. They were cowed into submission or obedience by a fear of this angry giant looming over them and shouting at them, so they employ it on their kids.

"Thus the habit of anger is passed from generation to generation. The same people may adopt anger as a control technique when they attain positions of authority. They rule by anger and by instilling fear in their subordinates. Sometimes they use anger to compensate in a perverse way, for the anger directed against them in childhood."

If you searched for years, I don't think you will find a true life story that so remarkably illustrates Dr. Russianoff's observations about anger as the one which follows.

Jeff, a Denver banker in his late forties and a divorced father of three grown children, is now happily remarried and acting as father and grandfather to his new wife's adult children and their youngsters. He describes how his own childhood came back to haunt him as an adult—and parent.

Jeff's Compulsion: Rage

"The lessons in discipline that I was taught were generally swift and severe. The verbal abuse was continuous. Many times my father would use the first object he could grab to issue my punishment. It didn't take much to set him off. He would go into incredible rages heightened by untreated diabetes and hypertension.

"My dad would discipline us by spanking us with a belt. If he got really upset, he would have a tantrum and he would use the belt buckle. I know there were times when my dad would get driven up on the high of an adrenaline buzz when he was disciplining us. This occurred a couple of times a week. I don't know if I've quite forgiven him for those times.

"When he was going to beat one of my sisters, I would step in the way. He would beat the hell out of me, but then he was too tired to hurt them. Once my dad beat me because I splashed some water on my sister while she was washing dishes. He tore off my shirt and started beating me. I wouldn't cry. I remember him jumping up and down, all three hundred and twenty-five pounds of him, beating me with the belt buckle. I was huddled on the floor, trying to cover up my head, and he was screaming, 'Let's kill him. Let's kill him.' I didn't give a shit at the moment if I died. I felt that would be better than where I was.

"In my teens, my only defense was not giving him the satisfaction of seeing me cry. I would take my beating and glare at him for doing it. My mother, though seldom a witness, would implore me to 'Just cry, so he will stop.' She said I had caused it to be more severe by being so defiant. I refused to acknowledge that it hurt me.

I got in lots of fights during junior and senior high school and into early adulthood. At twenty-three I was arrested and charged with fighting and disorderly conduct. When my father stopped beating me I simply found others who would because I thought I was no good and deserved to be beaten.

"Eventually, I became a parent. The way I was disciplining my children scared me one night to such depth and with such fervor that I called a telephone number for child abuse prevention displayed on the television. One especially frightening incident occurred when my six-year-old daughter had not come home from school and instead followed a friend home to play. I thought that something had happened to her and searched frantically until I found her. Then I kept yelling at her all the way home. When we got home I put her on the floor, put my knee in the middle of her back, pulled off my belt, and spanked her. She was screaming and terribly afraid. My wife was screaming at me and trying to pull the belt away from me. I just could not stop myself because I wanted to do it so much. Not only was I spanking her, but I was also spanking myself and feeling the fear that I felt when my dad was beating me with the buckle end of his belt while I was lying on the floor writhing in pain. The same damn thing was happening. I was dealing with my kids the same way my dad had dealt with me. I hate like hell to admit that I ever did such a thing, but I did it and it scares me even today. The abused child becomes the child abuser.

"The television public service announcement offering help to prevent child abuse helped me realize what was happening. In my daughter's eyes I could see the same bewilderment and fear that I had felt as a child at the hands of my father. I did not want her to fear me, the way I had feared my father. The commercial, 'Stop Child Abuse,' had a toll-free number to call. It was a moment of clarity. Immediately, I explained to my daughter that she had scared us and that I was glad she was safe with us at home. Later that evening, when the children were out of earshot, I called the child abuse hotline. They suggested a counselor for me, and I made an appointment.

The process was not easy. I was able to recount many episodes of anger and rage that I had experienced. During one session I asked, 'Why do I get so incredibly angry?' The counselor countered, 'You like the buzz.' The truth of her pronouncement really made sense. In the height of anger, I would have an adrenaline rush. Then, I would have an emotional hangover of depression and shame.

"Eventually, I was able to learn to respond to circumstances instead of instantly reacting. It took time and lots of counseling to learn new coping skills. I got involved with recovery groups that openly discussed similar experiences and new ways of dealing with life and emotions. My real problem, I learned, never was the anger, it was fear—but the only way I could deal with fear was anger. My response to fear was fight. I didn't know how to take flight.

"All I ever wanted was to have happy and healthy kids. In the past, when they got energetic and full of life, I told them, 'Shut up, sit down, and act right.' I wanted them to act like adults, but they're not adults—they're children. As a child, I was told the same thing. If my kids can be kids, the cycle can stop now. One of the most important things in my life is to be able to control my anger so my kids won't have the same issues to deal with that I have.

"Now, I can see how my behavior has an impact on others, good and bad. Sometimes situations trigger my anger, but I know if I am obnoxious and abusive, others will react to me the same way. The more cordial and helpful I can be to others, the more I will receive the same in return.

"I'm capable of growing and changing. I'm not doomed to remain the same. I can change and people around me can change. I stepped outside of my boundaries and found out that I was capable of bigger and better things. It feels good."

WHY DID I KEEP DOING THAT?

"Anger and denial were my only two coping skills. If I was afraid, remorseful, anxious, or depressed, I either denied it or made a show of anger, often rage. It was the way I knew. Through introspection, discussion, and many tears, I learned to identify my feelings, which I had always masked by denial and rage.

My Suggestions for Change

"I often mentor other men who learned the same limited set of coping skills. I ask them to stop and try to identify their feelings. I ask that they call me and I talk them through a rough time, if necessary. I help them learn that a measured response is much more helpful than an outrageous reaction. Denying a problem does not make it go away, and problems frequently become larger the longer they are left to fester.

"Positive action brings positive results. I have new feelings nearly every day, but I have a healthier and more positive way of dealing with them."

Like father, like son. In Jeff's case, it's like son, like father. From childhood through his teen years to his adult parenting years, Jeff became the living answer to Dr. Russianoff's questions and theories:

"What were we taught and how were we treated when we were growing up?

"What emotional models are we copying?

"We create our own emotional environment with our families, on the job, and among our friends. We can create a negative environment and wallow in it, or we can create a positive environment and succeed in it."

Our parents modeled their feelings for us whether they realized it or not. As much as we say, "I'm never going to be like my father," or "I'm never going to be like my mother," here we are today. As adults we often seem to be a mix of the best and worst of both of our parents.

I think I am. For all the negatives that may have come out of our childhood, all the positives we are came from the same childhood. I have to remember that and I try to every day.

I attended a workshop a couple of years ago. In one exercise I saw—or at least had it shown to me more clearly than I had ever seen before—that sometimes I can get very frustrated and be very aggressive, and at other times I become quite passive, exhibiting a "I really don't care about it at all" attitude. Where did all that come from? "Hello, Father; hello, Mother." A small example, but a major insight.

We may have "learned" our negative feelings in childhood and we may have been "practicing" them for a long time. However, in *When Am I Going to Be Happy?* Dr. Russianoff writes, "If they are habits, then there is hope, since habits can be broken."

To underscore a previous thought, it's our feelings about ourselves, the people close to us, the situations we encounter in our daily activities, and the big events that happen in the world that determine our level of happiness, contentment, and peace of mind.

Feelings Inventory

This following Feelings Inventory will help you identify not only what you feel but why you feel as you do, and importantly, where those feelings came from.

Review the powerful influences that your childhood had on your feelings. (For those who grew up influenced primarily by one parent, answer these questions with that single parent in mind.) There are no right or wrong answers. The purpose of this inventory is self-awareness, not self-judgment.

Were your parents optimists or pessimists? _____

_____

_____

_____

Would you characterize their general moods as happy or sad?

_____

_____

Were they gentle or angry? _____

_____

Relaxed or tense? _____

_____

Did your parents struggle? _____

_____

What were their attitudes about:

Sex?_____

Money?_____

Life?_____

Other people?_____

God?_____

Did your parents have many friends? _____

_____

_____

_____

In what ways are you like your mother? _____

_____

_____

_____

In what ways are you like your father? _____

_____

_____

_____

List three negative *behaviors* you do regularly that cause you to be self-critical. Is there a feeling you can attach to each?

Behavior: _____ _____ _____

Feeling: _____ _____ _____

Is there a reoccurring feeling? _____

Why do you think you do (or fail to do) each behavior or habit? Jot those thoughts down as well. _____

_____

_____

_____

_____

_____

List three general areas of your life that may be unsatisfactory to you. _____

_____

_____

_____

At the present time, list your three closest relationships. How do you feel when you are with each person? Write that feeling below each name.

Name: _____   _____   _____

Feeling: _____   _____   _____

In a quick review of all of your feelings answers, is there a single or dominant feeling that is pervasive? Is it related to a person, situation, or behavior? What negative feelings are you experiencing by staying attached to a particular situation, person, or behavior? Does fear or anger play a role in why you remain?

If you want to feel good, you may need to make a change, and you know what it is, don't you?

CHAPTER SIX

HARMFUL RELATIONSHIPS

The quality of our relationships is an important measure of our comfort zone and our self-worth. Those closest to us—mates, lovers, best friends, and family members—can enhance our sense of well-being through support, affirmation, care, time, and attention, or they can destroy our sense of value through criticism, unpredictability, lack of interest, lack of support, outright rejection, and physical, emotional, or sexual abuse. As children, we had little choice about who we tried to love and who was supposed to love us. As adults, however, we no longer have to stay with or put up with people who abuse us or do not treat us well. No parent, partner, family member, boss, co-worker, teacher, or friend has the right to treat us badly. If we are continually abused, the problem is ours because we are still "there" in the situation or relationship, and we are letting the abuse go on.

If we were raised in an unloving home, the compulsion to repeat dictates that we still need to be "told" we are unlovable, as our parents "told" us. The messages we received from our troubled parents were: "We don't love ourselves, we are unhappy, and you don't deserve to be loved or happy either." Often, negative and painful relationships give us the evidence we seek to support our "I-am-no-good" self-image.

Patrick, a dentist in his mid-forties, saw the light in a group therapy session I was observing: "I've always been attracted to negative people," he said. "It figures, look at the family in which I was raised. I've got to be very careful about those kinds of people. I've got to run in the other direction when negative people show up in my life—and they do. Maybe I attract them."

Just as Victoria related in Chapter 2, Patrick was aware that he was vulnerable to a certain kind of person, and now that he was aware of that—even to the point where he was willing to admit that there might be something he was putting out that attracted negative people—he had to be on guard not to fall into their trap of negativity.

There may be a lot of truth to the thinking that says the sadist and the masochist can find each other in a dark room full of five hundred people. This couple did. Jane, an elementary school teacher in Philadelphia, stayed with her husband, Rob, even after he told her he was having an affair. He also was a heavy drinker, admitted to using cocaine frequently, and wouldn't seek professional help.

Jane's Compulsion:
An Abusive Marriage

Jane spent most of her energy trying to stop Rob's unfaithful behavior, or talking on the phone about his alcohol and drug use with her girlfriend, Lynn. Rob, a moderately successful stockbroker, resented Jane's attempts to "control" him, but Jane "loved" Rob and felt he would change.

Jane had grown up with an alcoholic father. Rob, an only child, was raised by a single mother who demanded a lot from him emotionally. Jane counted on Rob's love for their two kids and her—in that order—to get him to seek help, even though his drinking, drug use, and affair were apparently more important to him than his family.

This painful relationship eventually brought Jane into counseling. In six months, she was able to understand on both an intellectual and emotional level that by putting up with Rob's infidelity and rejection, she had re-created the abusive and familiar family pattern of her childhood.

Her alcoholic father had not been emotionally present for her as a child. By not loving Jane as a parent should, her father not only rejected her, but also battered her sense of self-worth. Although she didn't know it at the time, Jane's primary motivation for her marriage to Rob was an attempt to "fix" her own past misery. She also sought to gain a sense of self-worth by rescuing Rob and changing him. Yet, she didn't realize that either.

By focusing on Rob, Jane was able to avoid experiencing the sadness, loneliness, and anger of her own unhappy childhood, and had an excuse for being unsuccessful in dealing with her weight problem. Of course, her failed relationship with Rob allowed her to identify with her own mother in the role of "victim married to an alcoholic." The circle, or pattern, was complete.

Jane and Rob were "made" for each other. Jane was the blame/victim champion and clung to her thinking that Rob and her father were the causes of her unhappiness. Jane's girlfriend, Lynn—in an inspired moment of best girlfriend advice—pushed Jane to see a marriage counselor.

I asked Jane about her relationship with Rob.

Why Did I Keep Doing That?

"I saw some of the warning signs when we dated back in college. Of course we all drank, but Rob drank more and more often than the rest of our gang. Looking back on it, I was naïve at best and blind at worst. He was an accident waiting to happen.

"I thought when we got married, he'd change, settle down, raise a family, and we'd live happily ever after. What do the kids say? Duh! I saw the same thing with my mom and dad. I asked my mother after my father died why she stayed with him with all of his drinking and yelling. Her answer was kind of beautiful in a sad kind of way. She said, 'Because I loved him.' I loved Rob too but I have more time on the planet, I'm tired, and I want something better for me."

My Suggestions for Change

"I guess the best piece of advice I can give to someone in a relationship like mine is to say that you can't change him. Never. Ever. Chances are also pretty slim that he will change himself; if he does change it's going to be his doing, not yours, and I'm sorry to say that it may not be with you. If it were with you—although Rob rejected the marriage counseling option with me—you'd both need a lot of help, individually and together.

"I've read—and it was a bitter pill for me to swallow, but it may have helped in the long run—that the person who stays with the addict/alcoholic/abuser is sicker than the person who has the more obvious problem. In some sick way, I guess I wanted the pain. Maybe I thought that the yelling, the unpredictability, the embarrassment, the heartbreak were just part of the marriage package.

"I thought I could change Rob but you can't change anybody but yourself."

To understand more about abusive relationships, I talked with Dr. Nathaniel Branden.

I asked him: Why does a woman who grows up in an alcoholic family marry an alcoholic?

"There are several desires that usually drive human behavior. One, to feel love; two, to avoid emotional or physical pain; three, to love in an active sense; four, to enhance self-esteem; and five, to achieve. Of course and unfortunately, they all contain the possibility for pathology. What we don't know is how a person will go about satisfying a particular desire. Some people will do terrible things to win love.

"Why does a woman who grows up in an alcoholic family marry an alcoholic? Perhaps it's an unconscious desire to win Mother's approval by being just like her; maybe she somehow formed the notion that this is what women do; or, if she had a sane, happy, well-balanced marriage, she'd become an outcast in her own family, since nobody else could relate to her. That last explanation is a powerful motivator for many people. To look for one simple explanation of why the woman would marry an alcoholic is already a mistake. We have to find out what need she's trying to satisfy with what she's doing.

"Good therapy will certainly improve her odds that she will succeed in changing her behavior. I'm interested in what it would take to change behavior.

"I would work on what sub-personality, what part of her, controls her love options or marriage choices. Is it the child? Is it the teenager? If it were her way of staying connected with her family, then, I'd work on her fear of being an independent person in the world and not a member of that family—all of whom are probably sick.

"Self-esteem can affect the quality of our judgment when it comes to those with whom we surround ourselves, or those we hire or choose to represent us. People can destroy their own chances for success or happiness or love by acting in self-defeating ways. We all know that people sabotage potentially promising love relationships; or at work, just when they're about to have a great success or get a promotion, they get their boss angry with them. It's self-destructive behavior of one kind or another. It happens all the time, unfortunately."

Jane was fortunate and received excellent therapy. Her counselor helped her realize that, although the two men in her life—Rob and her father—were in some ways the initial sources of much of her pain, it was her feelings, thoughts, behaviors, and decisions that fueled her abusive relationship. Jane's counselor challenged her to accept responsibility for her own life and suggested she create a life without conflict or pain, even without Rob if necessary, and Jane was willing to try.

The Jane/Rob relationship is a familiar one. Jane fears being left by Rob as her father emotionally abandoned her. She will go to any lengths to hold on to Rob, who is actually the source of her pain. On the other hand, Rob is afraid of being engulfed in a deeply committed relationship (remembering his mother's neediness), so he mistreats Jane and runs away when mature reciprocity is sought.

Relationships often fail because we pick the wrong person (for the wrong reasons), yet they develop because some needs are being met. However, childhood plays an essential role in determining our adult relationships. Too often, parents fall woefully short in meeting their parental obligation, which is to teach the child that he or she is good, lovable, capable, worthwhile, and important.

Masochism

What happens if children don't receive these positive messages from their parents? For answers, I talked with Dr. Natalie Shainess.

―――

Natalie Shainess, M.D.

HAS WORKED AS A PSYCHIATRIST AND PSYCHOANALYST
FOR OVER FIFTY YEARS. SHE HAS WRITTEN OVER TWO HUNDRED
PAPERS AND PROFESSIONAL BOOK REVIEWS AS WELL
AS THE BESTSELLING *SWEET SUFFERING*.

Dr. Shainess believes that if affirming messages were not given, the resulting negative effects on a child can be devastating. She introduces masochism as yet another possible explanation for our compulsion to repeat.

"Early experiences are imprint experiences. Largely, we repeat the experience of our own childhood. If your childhood had pain in it, it's going to be there again as an adult because you don't really know anything else. You certainly don't know what love and kindness are.

"Most adult human behavior depends on how we were treated as youngsters: how people were raised or not raised, or how people were abused—perhaps a more accurate description.

"Parents usually treat their children the way they themselves were treated, only worse. A parent who did not have a happy childhood is not likely to be a very good parent. Parents, when they get angry or when they're readily annoyed, can constantly be critical of the child. So where there's an ongoing adult problem, it's likely that it came about from something in childhood that has persevered.

"If a child knows nothing except punishment of one kind or another inflicted by parents, the chances are that he or she will create self-punishment as an adult.

"There is no question that masochism has its roots in childhood. Constant criticism from parents does more harm to self-esteem and self-worth than anything else. When a child who was constantly criticized grows up, he or she will get connected with someone who's constantly criticizing. These are things we don't really outgrow.

"Masochism is not necessarily overtly negative behavior. Sometimes, it's putting up with disrespect. That doesn't make for a good marriage, work relationship, or friendship.

"Masochism means that an individual is self-punitive. There's a fear of criticism. For instance, a married woman may live constantly in fear that her husband will criticize her, which he might. Criticism is what she's known all of her life, so she may even bring it on herself. It all depends on her treatment as she was growing up.

"The person who's always apologetic for his or her behavior is a masochist. Being overly polite is also an expression of masochism. It certainly reveals a person who's frightened of other people. Fear plays a big role. Self-criticism is often a conscious process while self-punishment is most often an unconscious process.

"You repeat what you experience. We do things over and over again because it's almost inbred, one could say. If the parent was not very loving, then as an adult the child docsn't really know what love is."

Both Jane and Rob believed the other was the source of their unhappiness. They stayed together because they were afraid of leaving, afraid of starting over, and most important, afraid of being alone.

Early in her counseling, Jane kept talking about Rob and how she believed that, if Rob would change, everything in her life would be fine. She focused on Rob rather than on her own pain and fears. However, at the end of nine months of therapy, Jane could see the harm she was doing to herself and her children by staying with Rob, who continued to act out. Jane finally understood that what she mistakenly labeled as her "love" was really her intense need to be humiliated, hurt, and degraded. She also learned that Jane needed to work on Jane.

Jane's fear of abandonment and sense of worthlessness caused her to try to control others because she feared their love would not be freely given. Although she had always feared that Rob would leave her, in the end it was Jane—because of her increased sense of feeling good about herself—who made the difficult yet necessary decision to go. She finally saw that Rob was unwilling to change and that there was a good chance he never would. Her new healthy sense of self-esteem demanded she get away from him. Ending her marriage offered Jane the chance to get involved with someone who loved himself enough to love her. Jane discovered that the pain of grieving and loss were bearable compared to the abusive pain she experienced in her marriage.

Recently, I ran into Jane at a party in Washington and she looked happy. She had lost some weight and the tension had vanished from her face. She told me she was dating a guidance counselor at a high school who, she said, "loves me very much and adores my children."

Jane worked hard in therapy. Leaving Rob was a courageous step. Today, she is with a man who respects her and treats her well. One of the most important things she has learned is that she is responsible for making herself happy. For most of her life, she thought it was someone else's job.

Genetics expert Dr. Dean Hamer says bad relationships can be habitual.

"Having bad relationships becomes a bad habit for some people for either of two major reasons: A person withdraws and doesn't communicate what she or he is really thinking, and doesn't let their emotions out. This leads to a lack of communication between partners, which is always fatal. The second reason is almost the exact opposite: He or she becomes completely emotionally dependent on the other person, and his or her values, worth, and life are dependent upon the relationship.

"When people find that they've had a series of bad relationships, the most common fault is to blame it on their partner and think, 'If I could just find the right person, I'd get along fine,' rather than finding the defect within themselves and changing their own behavior. It's similar to the person who gets drunk all the time and decides to change from wine to cognac, when what they ought to do is stop drinking."

Atlanta public relations executive Pam keeps dating younger guys—and ending up alone. Here's Pam in her own words.

Pam's Compulsion: Unavailable Partners

"Ten years ago, a therapist told me, 'You've been dating the same guy since you were fourteen years old—unavailable, unwilling, or incapable—sometimes all three.'

"So, here I am, alone again. As I look back, I can see Bill really wasn't in our relationship for the past year, maybe even longer. He never seemed to show much enthusiasm for being together. Mostly, he talked about him and I listened to his hopes, his dreams, his fears, and his problems. He never asked me about me.

"At the beginning it was great fun. He stayed over at my house almost every night, practically lived there. The sex wasn't great, but it was okay. I don't know when we flattened out—probably after about ten months—but God, we kept it going for almost three years."

Many times we don't trust or act on our feelings even when we read them correctly. Sometimes we don't like what our feelings are telling us, so we deny them and accept what is unacceptable. Pam explains.

"During the last year, I never felt Bill cared about us, but I went along with it. I guess I don't feel too good about me or I would have called it off myself a long time ago; but, of course, I didn't and neither did he.

"Did I see it coming? Yes and no. Yes, I knew there was no energy in our relationship. But no, because we had tapered off seeing each other and it seemed to work for both of us. In my job as a press agent, I get a lot of invitations to parties so we did go out together at least a couple of times a week. I guess he was not only my security blanket, but my trophy too.

"But there was no warmth, no excitement. We were like what I call 'the old dead couple' you see across the restaurant sitting silently together with nothing to say to each other, but they're together anyway. We must have looked like a younger version of them.

"I own my own business, travel a lot and have won some national PR awards. I'm pretty smart, but not too bright, I think, in this situation. I told a friend about a business trip Bill and I took together. We arrived in San Francisco after a flight from hell: lots of delays and a plane change because of a mechanical problem. One of my cases with some special publicity materials got lost. Bill went ballistic because, as he explained to me some hours later, he was tired. He told me that the time we spent trying to find the case slowed us down in getting to the hotel where he wanted to take a nap and shower before we met my client for dinner.

"Of course, I was the one who should have been upset. Remember that these were my materials that were lost and finally found forty minutes later. The case had been put on the wrong baggage carousel. The whole thing was an inconvenience to him.

"A friend of mine listened to the missing case story in disbelief and grilled me on why I had put up with his selfish behavior. She finally asked, 'Were you on drugs?'

"Why didn't I end it? I don't know. I thought I loved him. We had history together and some good times over four years. He was an anchor in my life. He was someone with whom I could touch base every day. He knew me and brought some fun into my life, especially at the beginning. I guess I thought it would return.

"I realize now that my fear of loneliness, getting older, having only a few close friends are all part of my stuff. I'm pretty content with just one person and a few other friends. So Bill's a big loss. But not the worst. The guy I dated before him ended so badly, the pain lasted for almost two years. I was a zombie. My girlfriend said, 'We know that these relationships aren't going anywhere, that they're not good for us, but they're like putting on an old coat that's comfortable.'

"Actually, this time I can truthfully say that I began to realize that I wasn't feeling comfortable in the relationship, so I don't know how it would have played out in the long run. I was beginning to speak up and tell Bill things along those lines.

"After a trip to Dallas, I remember, I told him that during the whole time we were there he never stopped talking and complaining. I actually said to him, much to my own surprise, 'You know, I'm a very successful person. I've traveled all over the world. I've represented a lot of important clients and you never ask me my opinion about anything. I don't understand it.' I was waking up. Maybe he didn't want to hear that, saw the end coming from me, and beat me to the exit.

"My friend, Linda, wanted to put bright yellow 'STOP/DO NOT CROSS/POLICE LINE' tape all around me. Her fear was that Bill would come around, we'd get together, and I'd jump right back into it.

"You know, I don't think so. I've made it a point to avoid him. I've learned a lot about me since we split. I've learned that it's not about him; it's about me. I picked him. Like the therapist said about the guys I dated, and I didn't get it: 'unwilling, unable, incapable—maybe all three.' Just like my father."

WHY DID I KEEP DOING THAT?

"In retrospect, I'd say that my self-esteem and personal confidence were so low that they dictated my choices in dating young guys. I was trying to shore up my self-worth trying to make them make me feel good.

"Since I see myself as an introvert who is attracted to extroverts,

I want their popularity to rub off on me. The problem however is that young people are pretty wrapped up in themselves, which often left me frustrated and angry. It was easy for me to call them self-centered, but the truth of the matter is it was where they were on the growing-up path. In the end I guess we're all self-centered to a degree.

"When I demand too much (control) or need too much (depend), sooner or later there will be a blowup and somebody is going to walk and in my case, it was always them. Recently, I thought that I may be feeling some guilt around actually being happy. I didn't see that in my own folks whose marriage was pretty much a struggle. Maybe deep down inside I have been thinking that relationships are supposed to fail. Perhaps by choosing who I did, I guaranteed my own success at failure. That's a scary phrase. Is that possible?"

My Suggestions for Change

"As far as offering some practical suggestions, the best one I can offer—and don't laugh—is to find a copy of the book *He's Just Not That into You* and read it. You have to get honest with yourself about what's really going on and stop living in a fantasy world. I guess that in some relationships where there is a big age difference things can and do work out, but I think that would be the exception, not the rule. For people like me I'd suggest a 'Ten Commandments of Relationships' with the rules all laid out. Rule number one would be: twenty-year-olds should be in relationships with twenty-year-olds, thirty-year-olds with thirty-year-olds, and forty-year-olds with only forty-year-olds.

"I'd encourage you to enlarge your circle and look for good friendships. It's not wrong to be seeking a loving relationship, but see relationships for what they are and realize that often a younger person does not know how to do what you want, give what you need, and say what you want to hear.

"If you are looking for attention, support, care, and concern, let that happen for you. Begin with dating someone your own age or who has at least significant relationship experience. Watch success come your way and enjoy it!"

Dr. Scott Twentyman had some very interesting things to say when I pushed the subject of bad relationships a little deeper: Why does a woman in an abusive relationship fail to see it—and if she does see it, why doesn't she "get it"?

"She might not see it because she grew up in an environment where that was the norm, and she doesn't even think to question it. The messages of her childhood may have been: Life is a struggle or men are abusive, but you have to have a man so you put up with it. You've got a pattern of behavior that you can see. What you don't see is what's driving it.

"Maybe she's doing it because she has grown up in an environment that says, 'A woman is worthless. A woman deserves this kind of treatment. A woman only has worth based on the man that she's with.' Another possibility is that her behavior could be driven by guilt feelings. Maybe her parents got divorced and she felt responsible.

Young children are egocentric. So, she might feel guilty that 'Mommy and Daddy got divorced, and it's because I'm a bad girl.' One way of dealing with that guilt is to arrange to have herself punished for it, so she seeks out various situations that cause her pain.

"However, we have to be careful not to get into blaming the victim. The woman in a series of destructive relationships may be seeking them, but nobody deserves to be treated abusively. In some ways, she is a victim, very much so, but we have to be careful not to suggest that she asked for the abuse or must have wanted it.

"It may turn out that this woman had a very masochistic mother who very clearly gave her the message that she had little worth and that her worth was derived from a relationship. The mother had terribly low self-esteem and had been involved in a whole series of destructive relationships herself that were modeled for her. She got the message, 'This is the way it's supposed to work,' and then she re-creates it. That got her, as you can imagine, into a whole variety of negative situations where she was taken advantage of. The work of therapy or analysis is to help her become aware of why she involved herself in that pattern of behavior."

What is the quality of your own primary relationship? If you are not involved in a primary relationship at this time, how about your relationships with the one or two people closest to you?

Let your mind go back to your childhood, perhaps five or ten years old, and picture the relationship between your father and mother. What is the predominant thought that comes to mind about your parents' relationship? What are you feeling? It may be amazing, surprising, or even frightening for you to realize how very similar your parents' past and your present actually are.

Family Dynamics

For additional insight into how parents' relationships can shape our own, I talked with Terence T. Gorski.

———

Terence T. Gorski, M.A.

IS A LECTURER, AUTHOR, EDUCATIONAL CONSULTANT, AND THERAPIST, AND THE FOUNDER AND PRESIDENT OF THE CENTER FOR APPLIED SCIENCES IN SPRING HILL, FLORIDA.

Your relationships of today were modeled for you in childhood by your parents. Mr. Gorski explains the characteristics of *healthy* families, the results of growing up in that type of environment, and how it affects our relationships as adults.

"In a healthy family, parents treat each other with dignity and respect, and children learn that relationships are a source of joy, comfort, satisfaction, support, and nourishment. The family is the refuge you go to when you are burned out from the world, have a problem, and need love, caring, and kindness. When the world chews you up, you can come back to the family, and you have a place where you can truly be yourself. The healthy family affirms the unique qualities of an individual and says it's okay to be you: 'I am interested in your pain. I'm interested in what you think. I'll tell you whether I think you're right or wrong, but I'm going to love you either way. I'm not going to abandon you. I'm not going to kick you out.' It's an unconditional relationship: 'I love you. You're my child. I love you for who you are.'

"The parents find joy and satisfaction in being with each other. Periodically, they experience problems or struggles. They view those things as temporary setbacks to the norm, which is a pleasant, satisfying, comfortable, and rewarding experience. Their relationship serves as a model for their children. In a functional family, the norm is peace, calm, comfort, and joy, periodically disrupted by problems that are temporary. Then it returns to the norm of being happy."

Dysfunctional Families

Contrast Mr. Gorski's characteristics of a healthy family with those of a troubled family and the unhealthy relationships awaiting individuals who grew up in unhappy, unpredictable, and unstable environments.

"As children we develop a range of usual experiences that become our psychological norm. If a child gets emotionally beat up every day by his or her parents, that becomes the norm. When that child becomes an adult and gets in a relationship and psychologically gets beaten up every day, that is normal and within his or her comfort zone. If there is no psychological abuse, such people don't know what to do. They feel uncomfortable, and unconsciously they set their partners up to reabuse, to redo what brings them back into their comfort zones.

"In a dysfunctional home, the child learns that relationships entail a difficult, painful struggle; they temporarily feel good but will rapidly crumble back into a difficult, struggling, and painful situation. The child learns that at five or seven or ten or fifteen years of age.

Children from dysfunctional environments often end up in bad relationships because they believe on a fundamental level, 'I'm not worthy of being loved, and the only way I can get somebody else to love me is to trick them into believing I'm someone that I'm not.'"

Addictive Relationships

According to Mr. Gorski, if you come from a dysfunctional home, chances are you may end up in an "addictive" relationship. Here he describes the partners and the dynamics of that relationship.

"An addictive relationship has an extremely independent and self-centered partner who is grandiose to the hilt and believes, 'I'm entitled to the world,' and an extremely dependent and other-centered partner who feels, 'I'm really not worth anything, and I need the sanction of another human being to survive.' The self-centered partner says, 'So here I am. The world ends at the tip of my nose. The only people who are worthwhile are people who reflect what I think I am.' The other-centered person comes along and is able to mirror back the image the self-centered person wants to see. The self-centered person is saying, 'As long as you're mirroring me in the correct way, I'm going to reinforce you like crazy and it's going to be bliss.'

"It works until the other-centered person runs out of steam one night and doesn't have enough energy to mirror back what is needed. The relationship is going to blow up. Addictive relationships do not necessarily have to have self-centered and other-centered partners, but it's the norm."

Characteristics of Addictive Relationships

Human beings desire an intimate primary relationship. However, in some cases, people are so lonely and so desperate that they sacrifice their own being and value toward that end. Relationships can enhance or demean self-worth. Destructive relationships may be on par with severe chemical addictions as the most painful experiences people can and do endure. Mr. Gorski enumerates and contrasts seven major characteristics of addictive relationships and healthy relationships.

"The first characteristic is a belief in magical, unrealistic expectations: 'If I get into a relationship with the right person, that person will fix me, and my whole life will be okay.'

"The second characteristic of addictive relationships is the desire for instant gratification. 'The most important thing in my relationship with you is your ability to blow my mind on demand. I am using you like a drug. Your job is to change my mood and make me feel good. If you do it now, I'm happy; if you are not able to do it now, I'm not.' In a healthy relationship, short-term pleasure is nice but the person has a long-term orientation: 'If the sex tonight isn't mindblowing, that's OK, it will be again in the future. If you're tired tonight and if you need space, that's OK. Your job is not to be my drug; your job is to be a human being with whom I interact.'

"Third, dysfunctional relationships are dishonest: 'I lie about who I am; you lie about who you are. There are certain things about me I can't tell you.' There are no-talk rules. Healthy relationships are rigorously honest. There's a commitment to full consciousness. In a healthy relationship, 'I know who my partner is from A to Z. I know my partner thoroughly and intimately, and I accept my partner fully.'

"The fourth characteristic of a dysfunctional or addictive relation-ship is compulsive control: 'I only am interested in the portion of you that can produce a good feeling in me. I'm not going to let you shift; I'm not going to let you move. You have to act in a certain way, damn it, or you're no good.' This is why addictive relationships are so often marked by a pattern of love-hate, love-hate, and love-hate. In a healthy relationship, there is voluntary and free-flowing cooperation: 'I'm with you because I want to be; you're with me because you want to be. I don't *need* you.' The addictive relationship stance is: 'I need you; if you walk out on me, I can't make it.' There's psychological coer-cion, and both people feel pressure. In a healthy relationship, 'If you decide to leave it will hurt, yes, but I'll survive.'

"The fifth characteristic is lack of trust: 'I don't really believe you love me; I don't really believe you care about me. I don't really trust you're going to be what I need when I need you to be it.' In a healthy relationship, there's rational trust: 'I trust you to be who you are. I like who you are. I trust you're going to be who you are. I don't distrust you.'

"The sixth characteristic is social isolation. In an addictive rela-tionship, the couple becomes the whole world and nobody else fits. In a healthy relationship, there's social integration. 'There are my friends, there are your friends, and there are the friends we have together.' People are welcome into the relationship.

"The final characteristic of an addictive relationship is a recurring cycle of pain. The cycle goes from intense pleasure to intense pain, into disillusionment, blaming, and then desperate attempts to make up. Intense pleasure: 'Boy, you blew my mind.' Intense pain: 'I'm really mad because you can't do it again.' Disillusionment: 'I guess you're not the person I thought you were,' or 'I'm not the person I thought I was.' Blaming: 'It's all your fault,' and then, 'No, maybe it's my fault; I've been a fool.' Then, there is desperate action to go to the other person and fix the relationship. The partners make up, the intense pleasure comes back, and they start the cycle all over again.

Intimacy

The goal of a primary relationship is intimacy. Perhaps it's a bit corny, but I once heard the word intimacy broken down as "in-to-me-see." Those words express a vulnerable invitation of closeness at depth. Maybe it's not so corny after all. Terry Gorski explains:

"Intimacy is a close, personal relationship between two people that reflects affection, love, and a depth of knowledge about each other. These two people share common individual characteristics and distinctive relationship characteristics, which causes an intermixing or interweaving of interests and activities. This results in the relationship assuming a high level of importance, value, and priority in each partner's life.

"This is because, first of all, there's a close, personal association. If intimacy's going to have a chance, two people have to spend time together. (One of the biggest problems with people who come in for marriage counseling is that they're never together.)

"Second, it's between two people.

"Third, it reflects affection and love. Affection means, 'I like you.' Love means, 'I care about you, and I'm concerned about your well-being on a very deep level.' Love is the genuine and sincere concern about the other person's well-being.

"Fourth, the couple shares things in common. There's a commonality of experience. They have similar interests in significant ways. There's a natural common foundation that allows each person to feel, 'I know you and I'm interested in you, and you know me and you're interested in me.' The frames of reference are close enough so that they don't have to get out of their own comfort zone in order to relate to each other.

"Fifth, there are also distinctive characteristics in the relationship. When the couple gets together, there are enough things that are new, novel, exciting, interesting, or intriguing. There are enough complementary characteristics in the relationship to make it work, which causes interests and activities to interweave. So, it's not just two individuals; the relationship evolves into 'we.' 'This is our thing; this activity exists because of us.' If either disappears, it won't be the same thing anymore.

"Sixth, the interweaving of activities results in the relationship assuming a very high level of importance, value, or priority to each person. What they do together is important, and valued. 'I choose to be with you over anybody else.'"

Infatuation

Psychologically opposed to healthy intimacy is painful and destructive infatuation, Terry Gorski continues:

"People can't create intimacy. When people say they can, it's erroneous. What they are saying is that they can engage in behaviors that increase the likelihood of affecting another person in a certain way.

However, if two people are emotionally mismatched, you can do all the right things and intimacy won't happen. The societal standard right now is to confuse the concept of infatuation with the concept of love. Infatuation is a state of temporary insanity that is marked by a sense of euphoria and the inability to see another person realistically. When you get infatuated, say to yourself, 'I am temporarily insane.'

"The basic mistake people make is to say, 'I've got to find someone to love.' What they mean is, 'I've got to find a victim for my love.'

"Infatuation is the intense feeling of physical and sensual attraction that leads to and culminates in sexual gratification. It is intense passion, plus intense sensuality and intense sexuality. People can have a long-term relationship based solely on infatuation, but it will be addictive. People become infatuated thinking that they're falling into love, and they're not satisfied. Something doesn't happen or is missing; there is emptiness. They don't get along and experience other problems, and the couple doesn't understand why.

"When all you have is infatuation, the partners don't love each other; rather, they love how they make each other feel. People get married for the wrong reason. People are taught to over-identify with the sexual.

"People coming out of a dysfunctional home always feel unlovable. They feel they have been loved for the role they play, not for who they are. You are only capable of re-creating with another human being the nature of the relationship you have with yourself. If you punish yourself, you will punish your love partner. If you hate yourself, you will end up hating your love partner. If you are afraid of yourself, you will be afraid of your love partner. A person is incapable of establishing a level of intimacy with another human being that is greater than the level of intimacy he or she has with himself or herself. You can't go out and find intimacy. What you can do is adopt a policy of attraction, and who you are limits who's going to be attracted to you. A person who needs to be victimized will attract an abusive partner. Healthy people attract healthy partners."

Successful Relationships

On successful relationships, Terry Gorski says:

"A number of years ago, researchers interviewed long-term married couples. The infatuation, passion, or intense love was found not to predict long-term success in marriage. As a matter of fact, marriages almost seemed more likely to survive in the long run if the initial passion was not too intense.

"The research does suggest that predictors of success were: shared levels of self-esteem; mutual expectation of autonomy and freedom; common interests, values, spirituality; common lifestyle preferences and complementary differences (does the person have enough intriguing differences to keep the interest and sparks alive?); and an active identification with some vision bigger than a person that gives life meaning and purpose."

Primary relationships that are noncaring, nonloving and nonaffirming usually involve two people who are heavily loaded with negative emotional baggage. The common bond is dependency, and each partner is probably using the other to shore up his or her own low self-esteem. Insecurity seeks out insecurity; low self-esteem connects with low self-esteem. What's the old adage? "Never play cards with someone named Doc, never eat at a restaurant called Mom's, and never sleep with someone whose problems are greater than your own."

If your primary relationship is filled with struggle, if you find yourself walking on eggshells, and if you are constantly working to hold your relationship together, then you already know your relationship is costing you a great deal.

Relationship Addiction and Change

Terry Gorski offers some final thoughts on relationship addiction and some suggestions about change:

"A relationship addict is a person who compulsively seeks excitement in a relationship. The relationship addict needs the intense emotionality of an intimate, mind-blowing, and passionate relationship. Some 20 to 30 percent of adults are hooked on chronically addictive relationships. The figure is higher for younger people.

"People involved in an addictive relationship can change. They need to declare abstinence from high-risk addictive partners. What I'm suggesting is that you identify the type of person you get involved with addictively and avoid that type like the plague. High-risk partners can be difficult to spot. Sometimes there's no common denominator in physical appearance or physical behaviors; high risk can be defined by the kind of people they are or perhaps the lifestyle they live. The relationship addict is addicted to the feeling the other person creates inside. Certain types of people create the rush they desire. Abstinence means living without the rush.

"Begin getting involved in casual, superficial dating relationships with the type of partner whom you would usually find dull and boring. Make a decision to date without making any significant commitments. Always date at least two people at a time and abstain from sex for the first three dates. There should be no exchange of money, and you should not live together for at least three months. Build the relationship slowly. Keep it superficial.

"Before you spend significant time alone, observe the person and see how he or she interacts with other people in your presence. Go to parties and see what they do. Slowly reveal a little bit more about yourself and see how the other person handles it. Go to the next step and share more and more intensive, exclusive activities. Then begin spending time where you're alone without the protection of other people or structures. Then move to the final step where you share progressive intimacy. Do it responsibly with no dishonesty.

"If two partners are involved in an addictive relationship and they're married, they have to abstain from the behaviors that create the super highs and the super lows. That may mean a break from sex. It may mean taking a vacation from each other. The decisions get more difficult.

"For anyone who is in an addictive relationship, the chances of working it out without professional help are slim to none."

If our relationships and friendships make us feel good, lovable, capable, worthwhile, and important, we are probably living a fairly active, productive, and happy life. If the people in our lives are not committed to our growth, security, and happiness, and are sending us the negative messages—you're not good, not lovable, not worthwhile, and not important—the effect will be devastating.

Relationship Inventory

If you are in a primary relationship, the questions in this Relationship Inventory may help you to evaluate how your partner supports or negates you. What are the messages of your primary relationship? The answers also speak volumes about your self-worth and comfort zone. If you are not currently in a primary relationship, apply these questions to your closest friend or family member.

Do you feel loved?	❏ Yes	❏ No
Are your needs being met?	❏ Yes	❏ No
Do you feel respected?	❏ Yes	❏ No
Is your relationship pleasurable?	❏ Yes	❏ No
Is there a conflict in your relationship?	❏ Yes	❏ No
Is the problem yours?	❏ Yes	❏ No

What can you do about it? _____

_____

_____

_____

_____

What are your options? _____

_____

_____

_____

Have you sought help for yourself?   ❏ Yes   ❏ No

Are you afraid of leaving?   ❏ Yes   ❏ No

Why do you stay? _____

_____

_____

_____

_____

If you must go, what will be the result of your leaving this relationship? _____

_____

_____

_____

_____

In order to lead a richer, fuller, and happier life, we may need to get out into the people store and do some shopping.

Perhaps in the last month or so, you met someone who you liked instinctively. Will you risk asking that person to have dinner, lunch, a drink, or a cup of coffee? Will you make it a goal to try to add one new person to your circle of friends over the next few months, weeks, or days?

CHAPTER SEVEN

HOW IT WORKS

The engine driving our current choices and actions are our feelings, shaped years ago. When we were children, we learned all kinds of coping mechanisms to make it through the ups and downs of family life. We knew what our parents would do to get what they wanted, and we developed the moves that we had to make in order to survive. Problems may surface, though, when we take our childhood coping skills and ways of getting our needs met into the rest of the world—outside our families. These new people will not play by the same set of rules and regulations. That being the case, our "solutions"—as Dr. Twentyman calls them—that used to work, just don't work any longer.

Unintended Consequence
of a Failed Strategy

For more insight into what drives our choices and actions, I talked with Dr. E. Virginia Demos.

E. Virginia Demos, Ed.D.

IS ASSISTANT CLINICAL PROFESSOR OF PSYCHOLOGY AT
HARVARD MEDICAL SCHOOL AND A MEMBER OF THE MEDICAL STAFF OF
THE AUSTEN RIGGS CENTER IN STOCKBRIDGE, MASSACHUSETTS.

Dr. Demos introduces us to the important work of Silvan S. Tompkins, a noted philosopher turned psychologist. While Freud believed his pleasure/pain principles as well as sex and aggression "drives" were keys to the human motivation system, Dr. Tompkins believed it was our emotions. Dr. Demos presents Tompkins' principles and then offers us an example of how feelings play out in the life of one woman—from childhood to adulthood.

"Although it is puzzling to see a person do something over and over again or adopt behaviors that seem, from the outside, so self-defeating or painful, my assumption is—as bad as it seems for the person—there must be something worse that they avoid feeling by doing what they're doing.

"They're not seeking pain, not trying to hold on to a past destructive caregiver, not trying to master painful feelings; they're trying to make it work. When you see a repeating pattern of people ruining things, of getting a great job and then spoiling it for some reason, and getting another seemingly great job and then messing that up, or having one boyfriend after another or never being able to get into a relationship at all—it is self-defeating and destructive. The result is the unintended consequence of a failed strategy.

"With Tompkins, the bottom line is that we prefer to feel better than not to feel better. We're always trying to feel the best we can, even if it means that sometimes we're in pain.

"Silvan Tompkins believed that emotions were the core of our motivational system. He argues that emotions make good things better and bad things worse, because they essentially function as an amplifier, and their purpose is to make you care about whatever is happening.

"Emotions or feelings are innate programs. You don't have to learn them. The newborn baby doesn't have to learn how to cry when hungry or angry. Anything that happens afterward is going to be learned as something that goes with that feeling. For instance, the infant learns that 'When I cry, something happens afterward.' The caregiver comes, soothes the infant, and either feeds it or provides whatever the infant needs at that time. The infant learns from that sequence. 'I cry and this happens.' In a well-functioning home, by two or three weeks, an infant will stop crying just at the sight of the caregiver coming, because the child has learned, 'When I'm hungry and I cry, someone comes, comforts me, and feeds me.'

"What Tompkins would say, first of all, is that feeling is a momentary phenomenon. It simply amplifies whatever is happening in that moment and we don't live by that alone. We bring all of our resources to bear on the events or scenes we experience. We assemble them, consider their relationship to each other, and design strategies to deal with them in the future. Tompkins called this a 'set of compressed rules' and labeled them 'scripts.'

"Tompkins believes you begin to relate scenes that feel alike, and as you begin to do that, you start to design a way to manage those scenes. So when you experience something in the present moment that feels familiar you might say to yourself, 'Ah, this is another one of those moments. This is like what I felt when X, Y, or Z happened.' When you do that, you magnify both of those scenes—the present one and the one from the past—and they become more like each other. Magnification occurs over time, creating a family of scenes that are similar in their feeling quality. A scene usually has some kind of trigger to it, which could be a feeling, an interpersonal interaction, an event, or just about anything.

"According to Tompkins, the scene is the basic unit of psychic experience. As negative scenes increase, they begin to form a little family of scenes and a person develops a set of rules that says, 'I don't want this to happen. I have to devise a strategy either to prevent this from happening or find a way to get out of it.' Tompkins related specific scripts for specific emotions or feelings. His list of feelings includes: enjoyment, interest, distress, anger, fear, startle, disgust, and shame.

"To understand Tompkins' theory and how it works, let me focus on one feeling and one script and follow it through a person's life.

"Let's look at what Tompkins called the decontamination script, which is related to the feeling of disgust. You eat something that looks good and smells okay, at least initially, but as you eat it, it turns out to be bad and you have to get rid of it, to vomit. That's a physiological disgust reaction."

"Metaphorically, disgust is a response to disenchantment in which both the 'dis' and the 'enchantment' are important elements. You have to become enchanted first with something, and then you find out that it's really painful or hurtful in some way, and your wish is to get rid of it—or to decontaminate and purify yourself—in some way."

Childhood

Dr. Demos shows us how early negative scenes can set the stage for failed strategies later on.

"For example, a toddler is building a tower out of blocks with a parent. The child makes a mistake and the tower falls down. It starts out as an experience of enjoyment and interest—a child and parent doing something together. When the tower falls, the parent suddenly becomes quite punitive, calls the child a critical name, and says sarcastically, 'You can't do anything,' and walks away and abandons the child. So something that started as a good experience has now been spoiled and the child feels awful—helpless, bad, and needing the parent even more. And if the child gets angry at such times and is rejected for this anger, the sense of badness is even more magnified. That's a typical 'contamination' scene. Remember, however, such a scene has to be repeated for it to become a major script for a person and that can happen in many ways.

"Let's say at three years old, the child starts drawing something and the parent says, 'Let me help you with that,' or 'This is the way you draw a tree.' Pretty soon the parent has taken over and the child is left watching as an observer.

"When the child feels that negativity, the child feels inept and abandoned by the parent and may think, 'I am not worth anything.' So, there's a back and forth between dreading that and imagining it's the worst and the most horrible thing in the world.

"Once she is into this script, as a child, the goal is to try to seek perfection. She might get into trying to do everything right so she doesn't get a demeaning, shaming, or disgusted reaction from the parent, or isn't abandoned and left alone with self-loathing.

"The child imagines that if she does everything perfectly, she will be loved. She has bought that bill of goods from the parent. The parent acts as if to say, 'If you weren't so stupid or so displeasing, I could love you.' The message is, 'Why can't you do better? Why can't you do what I want you to do so I can love you and want to be with you?' In the child's fantasy, everything will be fine if she does it right, and she believes 'It's all my fault that everything isn't fine.'

"There's a definite maximizing/minimizing strategy that develops where she imagines that she could actually live a life or perform in such a way that she would never be criticized in any form, because criticism becomes so painful and so catastrophic that it plunges her into a pit of self-loathing.

"Suppose when the child is older she scores a goal for her soccer team. The child feels excited, but then the parent starts to tell everybody, 'I've got this terrific kid. She scored that goal. I used to be a pretty good player myself and my kid is really going to be the best player.' Suddenly it's not the little child's goal anymore. The parent has taken over, and now the child's got to perform more and more. God forbid the child doesn't score another goal or score a goal in the first place.

"It's not a horrible crisis, but the parent has usurped the child's victory for the parent's own aggrandizement and pleasure. It's not the child's anymore. The child is held to such a high standard, she can't dare fail. Even positive accomplishment gets 'spoiled' in some way.

"Yes, that feeling of 'I can't stand this spoiled feeling. I've got to get rid of this.' That's the disgust feeling of basic rottenness. The child doesn't have the capacity to step back and say, my parent is really exaggerating and is way out of line here. No child has the capacity to do that."

It is important to underscore the point Dr. Demos has just made. Little children do not have the ability and facility to accurately judge their parent as being wrong, self-centered, selfish, troubled, or disturbed—let alone say anything in defense of their own behavior. If there's a divorce or when a child is the target of parental physical, emotional, or sexual abuse, the child often blames himself or herself, thinking 'I did something to displease my father (or my mother) and I am wrong.'

Dr. Demos continues with the dynamics of this troubled parent-child relationship.

"The essential ingredients that lead to this script are first of all, the seduction: some quality in the parent that communicates, 'I really care about you.' The parent is intensely invested in the child, projecting a lot of his or her expectations on the child the parents have produced. There is little or no toleration of any sign of badness in the child. The child's imagination is seized with the wish to please, to join, to be close to this idealized other who presents himself or herself as, 'I'm what you ought to try to be like.'

"This is combined with a second essential element: the inevitable failure to comply with the parent's needs, not validating the parent's goodness, or irritating the parent in some way, and the parent exaggerating the child's failures, again and again. Some upset parents will say, even to very young children, if the child has broken something, 'How could you do this to me?' The child didn't do anything to the parent, but the message—'How could you do this to me?'—is a huge weight, which has now impacted the child's life. The child feels he or she has done a terrible thing, doesn't quite know what is so bad about it, and feels confused, hurt, helpless, angry, and needy—all of which have to be suppressed, devalued, and disowned in order to get 'love.'"

Workplace

Dr. Demos reveals the painful adult consequences of perfectionism:

"As an adult this weight can play out in a number of ways. She will be afraid to make any kind of mistake. At work she may be afraid that her boss will fire her if she makes the slightest error. She might work incredibly hard and be very anxious every moment that any kind of fault might be detected in her performance. It can be a very stressful situation, depending on how intensely she's caught up in it. She'll be able to look around and see that other employees make mistakes and they're not fired or even reprimanded, but it just doesn't compute for her. That is not her reality. In a roomful of employees, several people will make stupid comments. Nobody laughs, but nobody mocks them either, and the boss keeps talking. In her mind, she has to make the perfect comment or she will be decimated. That's what she carries around in her head. So her need to be the perfect employee is the strategy that she has created to deal with her feelings of failure and inadequacy—to deal with not being plunged into a pit of self-loathing.

"Of course, when she does make a mistake and the boss may say something, she will experience it as a catastrophe and will be mortified. And even if nobody says anything, she's intolerant of her own perception of her lack of perfection. She may try to laugh it off as something light, but she is struggling with her commitment to perfection. It's torture for her, and it may mean that she becomes so paralyzed she can't even work."

Relationships

Dr. Demos examines the effects of this "commitment to perfection" in the woman's personal life:

"In her adult personal relationships she'll hide various things about herself; she'll be very anxious that someone might know too much about her or get too close to her. It will be difficult for her to become intimate with people, because then they would know awful things about her. At the moment when people get really close, she might start to push them away. She wants closeness, but she doesn't want anyone to get too close because then they'll see how awful she really is.

"There's a deep ambivalence about approaching and avoiding, because to get close is to know what a piece of crap she imagines she is. She has exaggerated her badness and exaggerated the degree to which she has to be good to get any kind of human contact or any kind of pleasure out of life. The result is the unintended consequence of a failed strategy.

"She's not seeking pain or trying to alter anything. She's trying to be perfect. Her thought is: *If I just give enough, maybe the other person will eventually notice me, want me, and love me.'* Usually the other person just keeps taking. Self-loathing people get into relationships like that.

"The truth is to know one's needs; to imagine that you have legitimate needs that are negotiable is a primary goal of life and relationships. You want to get to a point where you can say, 'I need to do this. You need to do that. How can we negotiate that so we each get something out of this?'"

According to Dr. Demos, the woman has developed "strategies" in the workplace and in her personal life to deal with her low self-worth. She has developed and adopted a way of navigating through life that suggests that nothing ever goes wrong. Her strategy of perfection is a failed strategy. It's bound to fail, and when it does fail, she goes back into self-loathing.

People in this script, according to Dr. Demos, can't even seem to look at their weaknesses and shortcomings because they feel their failings are so big, they can't possibly be repaired or changed. They exaggerate their badness and the only thing that gets them out of their despair is the next job or the next relationship, thinking, "I'll do it better next time and then it won't happen."

Seeking Help

Dr. Demos has some additional thoughts about self-acceptance.

"What causes people like her to seek help? Sometimes it's loneliness, a failure of a number of relationships, the inability to work, or a fear of their own rage. They don't trust themselves or they're scared they're going to hurt somebody else or even themselves.

"The middle ground of possibilities seems outside their experience. A therapist needs to point out this black-and-white world and the lack of a middle realm of experience. Little by little they will begin to see what they're doing; but it's a very slow, gradual process of exploring past experiences.

"Beginning to see patterns, recognizing black and white, and being able to accept one's limitations without becoming devastated by them is the hardest part because many people exaggerate their limitations. To get near them is a major task of therapy. Beginning to get them to look realistically at both their abilities on the positive side and their liabilities or vulnerabilities will eventually lead them to grieve all the things that didn't happen when they were growing up, like the childhood they never had.

"We all have bad parts. It's just that other people have learned that they're not so bad; it's what makes us human. On the other hand, some people have learned that their bad parts make them unacceptable. They can't face that. It's not really any worse than anybody else's bad part; it just was turned into something totally unacceptable. For them, it's being some awful, despicable somebody. In their eyes, they aren't human beings.

"In truth, no one is responsible for all the bad things that happen, nor is anyone responsible for all the wonderful things that happen. There's a limitation to the things any of us have any real control over. That's a hard thing to learn and let go of, because many people have grown up believing that they are responsible for everything. That's not humanly possible. Nobody has that kind of power."

The repetition of our negative behaviors temporarily makes us feel better and dulls our feelings of inadequacy, insecurity, anxiety, fear, hopelessness, and pessimism. In our often dependent relationships, we seek the acceptance and validation we are unable to give to ourselves or receive from others.

Identify the Inner Conflict

Your problem is not about the food. It's not about the alcohol. It's not about the cigarettes. It's not about the money. It's not about the work. It's not about the anger, the relationship, the pessimism, procrastination, isolation, self-doubt, or sex. They're only the symptom. If it's happening again or you did it again, it's time to look deeper.

Critical for making the dramatic change you seek is to identify a pervasive pattern, which probably shows up in many areas of your life. Hopefully coming into focus for you may be an understanding about your own behavior—not merely related to a specific symptom, but an insight more universal in scope affecting your very being.

Long-term success in stopping unwanted patterns and gaining rewards and benefits in all areas of your life is predicated on identifying the inner conflict driving the behavior that is generating negative feelings and making a total commitment to overcoming the compulsion to repeat it.

Uncovering the root cause or causes of our painful, harmful, and self-defeating behaviors, relationships, and feelings is our goal. The specific answer, of course, will be different for each of us.

Change is difficult and requires the willingness to create a new life. Change is possible. You can do it.

CHAPTER EIGHT

COURAGE TO CHANGE

Your tooth aches, your stomach hurts, your feet are swollen, you can't sleep at night, your lower back is killing you, your hands shake, you're bleeding—they're all physical symptoms. Something is wrong.

You keep gaining weight, yelling at your kids, losing money in bad investments, having unsafe sex, paying over-limit fees on credit cards, being late for appointments—they're all symptoms, too.

Physical symptoms hopefully cause some kind of immediate remedial action; you take aspirin, visit a doctor, or go to the hospital. Emotional and behavioral symptoms call for action too. The unhappiness you feel and the struggle you experience give you information just as important as any physical symptom. Here's a personal case in point, which illustrates that the seeds of change often have their roots in everyday circumstances.

One night several friends and I were sitting around talking about life's journey and what we had learned along the way. My friend Jimmy was speaking, and, since I always liked what he had to say, I shifted gears and listened a bit harder. He said the most important lesson he'd ever learned was, "Don't push the river." As soon as he said it, my attention drifted away from the group. "Don't push the river"—those few words seemed to summon up a hidden piece of what had been the very core of my life for so long. At that moment I began to see that so many of my "heroic" efforts over a lifetime—demanding perfection in myself and others, not taking "no" for an answer, pleasing the wrong people, trying so hard to make things work out the way I thought they should, and banging my head against so many walls were all ways I had engineered to keep struggle, stress, and anxiety running my life.

Extreme stress is the normal state of being if you grow up in a deeply troubled home, so I created my own stress as an adult. Sure, life is often difficult, but I know now that I re-created struggle in my life as a legacy of my past. I became very accomplished at swimming upstream ("pushing the river"). Struggle was what I grew up with, what I knew. I believe I actually became addicted to the struggle.

To pursue goals, dreams, and ambitions is exciting. Yet, I've learned that a lot of life is hearing the word "no" in one form or another. Consequently, to chase after the unobtainable in love, work, and play is "pushing the river." It has taken a lot of insight, work, and time to learn not to push the river. And I am still learning.

Struggle showed up in many areas of my life. I know that I would not have seen that as clearly as I do today if my therapist had not introduced me to the repetition compulsion.

Here's a minor but "successful" example of how I managed to create stress and anxiety for myself. I had developed a ritual, which I stopped a few years ago, and it wasn't funny anymore. When I was ready to leave home, I would spend three, four, or five minutes looking for my wallet and keys. It's a small behavior that was also conveniently tied to another of my shortcomings: being habitually late. Being late, of course, creates plenty of stress for any of us. I would beat up on myself in transit, arrive at my destination on the defensive for keeping others waiting, and then lower my self-esteem, apologizing for my tardiness.

I finally realized it wasn't simply about the keys and wallet and being late.

Punishing myself with plenty of negative self-talk for doing something so "stupid" as losing my keys and wallet was easier to identify than the always being late piece.

Although I've been on television in front of hundreds of thousands of viewers each week for an entire career, it began to dawn on me one day that in small social situations my real issue was intimacy. I know myself well enough now to admit that I frequently feel uncomfortable, out of control, and extremely vulnerable in close, personal encounters. Being late cuts down the necessity of small talk, which I believe I don't do very well. Being late also suggests some exaggerated sense of self-importance at the expense of others.

I am working on all of these with some very positive results. My keys and wallet are put on my desk every time I walk into the house, so now I know where they are when it's time to go. My clocks are set ten minutes fast and I am making it a point to arrive early for professional gatherings and social activities. I find that I am showing up more relaxed and even having some fun as I learn the art of making casual small talk. Now if I can just stop forgetting to take my glasses. . . .

It's very easy to blame where we are today on a less than perfect upbringing. Even the best of families with the best of parents have their failings. However, we can create our own troubles as adults without any help from them, thank you very much.

Jack, a friend of mine in broadcasting, recently was bemoaning the fact that he weighed one hundred eighty-seven pounds, recalling that he only weighed one hundred fifty-five pounds when he was in college. Although he was clearly beating on himself, his rationale was that wearing a tire around the middle was pretty normal at his age. He even argued (blaming genetics plus age, I guess) that his dad had gotten heavier as he got older. Left to present his own case, I'm sure that Jack would say that his mother—and now his wife—fed him too well or made too many tasty desserts. No puns intended, but Jack served up enough blame and put enough justification on the table to get himself off the hook—in his own eyes. But excuse me, Jack is an adult, and Mom, Dad, and wife didn't eat the food that caused those extra thirty-two pounds.

At some point we've got to get honest with ourselves, accept responsibility for where we are today, and take the necessary steps to get to where we want to go. If Jack really wants to lose twenty or thirty pounds, it's his job.

Accepting Responsibility

To learn more about where responsibility intersects with compulsions, I talked to Dr. Brad Blanton.

Brad Blanton, Ph.D.

HAS WORKED FOR MORE THAN TWENTY-FIVE YEARS AS
A PSYCHOTHERAPIST IN WASHINGTON, D.C. HE IS THE AUTHOR
OF *RADICAL HONESTY* AND CONDUCTS RADICAL HONESTY
WORKSHOPS THROUGHOUT THE COUNTRY.

Dr. Brad Blanton cautions that the "disease" concept of addiction may be a rationalization to avoid holding people accountable for the consequences of their behavior. He advocates accepting personal responsibility for our actions and suggests that to change any unwanted behavior, the first steps may be as obvious as paying attention and being aware of what we are doing.

"A lot of human behavior is determined by what we're avoiding. We're avoiding the re-feeling of those experiences we ran away from a long time ago. Everybody does this. All of us pretend a lot and most of us pretend that we're not pretending. That's where we get into trouble. The whole thrust of my work is to bring people into conscious awareness and to get them to practice radical honesty with themselves and with others. Attention is what we need for salvation.

"I remember sportscaster Howard Cosell interviewing Billie Jean King after she'd won Wimbledon for the third time. She'd won in straight sets, and she was incredible. So Cosell said, 'Well, Billie Jean, how did you do it?' Billie Jean was still in the groove, looked at him and said, 'OK, Howard, I'll tell you, but don't interrupt me. Here's how I did it.'

"'When I got up this morning, all I did was get up. When I got out of bed, all I did was get out of bed. When I got dressed, all I did was get dressed. When we drove down here to the center, all I did was ride. When I went in to change clothes, all I did was change clothes. When I was tying my shoes, all I was doing was tying my shoes. And, when I went out there on the court and played tennis, all I was doing was playing tennis.'

"It was the first time I'd ever heard an honest answer to a sportscaster's question about some spectacular event. She just described what she was doing while she was doing it.

"There's something about actually *noticing* what you're doing rather than figuring out *why* you're doing it that allows you to actually interrupt a repetitive pattern. It allows you to be present in the experience of what you're doing at the moment, every second you're 'at choice' about being in control of what you're doing."

Pay Attention

Dr. Blanton continues:

"Timothy Gallwey's book *The Inner Game of Tennis* is eloquent in its simplicity. He says there are always two 'selves': Self One is the one who knows everything there is to know about playing tennis, and Self Two is the one who can play tennis if Self One can get out of the way.

"About a dozen years ago, I attended one of his talks. He showed a video clip of a television show hosted by Harry Reasoner, called "The Challenge," I think. The staff would read claims that people made in their advertising or their books, confront them with the claim, and then ask them to prove it. They landed on Gallwey because he claimed that he could teach anyone to play tennis in twenty minutes.

"At a little seaside resort in Southern California, they brought in one hundred sixty people and Reasoner's staff interviewed them to select the person to be the 'anyone' to learn tennis. Their choice was a large woman in a muumuu. She said that standing up to turn on the television set was the most athletic thing she had ever done.

"In the clip we viewed, Gallwey and the woman were on the tennis court. The woman was not wearing shoes. Tim said, 'We're going to do this thing called 'bounce, hit.' That fellow on the other side is going to throw a tennis ball over the net. When it bounces, we're going to say 'bounce.' When I hit it with the racket, we're going to say 'hit.' The guy starts throwing the balls and Gallwey starts saying 'bounce, hit, bounce, hit.' He says, 'Say it with me.' She starts saying, 'bounce, hit, bounce, hit.' Then he says, 'Okay, keep going,' and he hands her the tennis racket. She takes it the same way he held it and starts hitting the ball back. She's still focused on saying 'bounce, hit.' She misses the first one, but she still says 'bounce, hit' and hits the second one. 'Bounce, hit' and hits the third one. Eventually, she's hitting the ball back over the net, but she's still only thinking about saying 'bounce, hit, bounce, hit.' Tim takes the tennis ball and says, 'Okay, now we're going to do 'tah-dah, dah.' So, he throws the ball up for a serve and he says, 'tah-dah,' and as he hits it, he says, 'dah.' He hits seven or eight serves, hands her the tennis racket and the tennis ball, and says, 'Okay, keep going.' She goes 'tah-dah, dah.' The first time she hit a serve, it went over the net into the court.

"At the end, there was a volley sequence that lasted for a minute and a half, with Tim Gallwey on one side of the court and the woman on the other. They showed it in slow motion, and she was just beautiful. She was as graceful as a gazelle. She was glowing and beautiful. Her face was full of joy. It was incredible what he was able to do without ever giving a single instruction about what to do. Never once did he engage her Self One that knows everything about what ought to be done. Never once did he ever tell her what she should do. Never once did he ever say, 'Do it this way.' All he did was say 'bounce, hit, bounce, hit, tah-dah, dah.'

"All he was doing was directing her to pay attention to what was going on. That's where power resides for people to bring about a transformation: Pay attention to what's actually happening now. It's that awareness that allows us to actually interrupt repetitive behavior."

Change is difficult of course, but others have left bad relationships, quit dead-end jobs, filed for bankruptcy, entered a treatment center, asked for forgiveness, made apologies, gotten married, had children, quit smoking, lost weight, lost parents, conquered anger or jealousy, and traveled from negative to positive, from fear to faith, from hostility to hospitality. A few can do it alone, some work with a therapist or counselor, and others use support groups.

Money issues come up frequently in the arena of self-destructive behavior. It's a handy prop. People can do a real number on themselves thanks to easy-to-obtain credit and credit cards. Craig, a New York City actor who has recently enjoyed some success in TV commercials, is definitely someone who was affected by his childhood environment. Show business is about as tough a career as there is. The competition is fierce, and it's often months between jobs, so handling money wisely and with discipline is a necessity. Craig has wrestled for years with money problems.

Craig's Compulsion: Debt

"A couple of years ago, I had an awakening. It occurred to me that I repeat the same patterns and experiences with money over and over again—all leading me on a downward spiral of financial debt and mismanagement. I live month to month. I continually spend more than I make and increase my debt. I wait until the last minute to pay my bills and then scramble desperately to meet my commitments. I rob Peter to pay Paul. Or, if I am making steady money, I invariably face or create some huge expense, be it taxes, medical expenses, or some other unforeseen bill to whisk away my newfound cushion. Consequently, I end up feeling worried, anxious, and afraid, peeking out of one eye at the mountain of debt I am creating and feeling an overwhelming sense of doom and hopelessness about how I'm going to handle it. I have spent my life trapped inside a box with walls comprised of debt, anxiety, and scarcity. And I want out."

Craig has made some solid progress during the past year and tells us how he went about it.

"Last year, I spent a great deal of time trying to understand the first step toward change—by examining how I thought about money and how my thoughts create the financial picture of my life. I realized it was my parents' fears and struggles with money that shaped my own patterns. My mother has spent the better part of her life worrying about money—where it was coming from and how we were going to manage our family's bills. I consistently heard her say 'We can't afford it,' 'Money doesn't grow on trees,' and 'I don't know what we're going to do (about money).' My mother's attitudes about money molded my own, but I'm not blaming her. I accept complete responsibility for my financial situation.

"Oh how I wish I could tell you that I turned around my financial situation and I am now independently wealthy! What I can tell you is that I am in a process of shifting some deeply ingrained attitudes, such as: *There is not enough, I will always have to scramble to make ends meet, I am not worthy of making enough money to be financially independent.*

"In the place of those negative messages, I now tell myself: *There is enough, I can afford it, I deserve the money I want to make.* I tell myself these things over and over again so that these thoughts are as deeply ingrained as the others were. Today, I choose to focus on abundance and prosperity. And I can see the fruits of this work. The bedrock of my former belief system is finally crumbling.

"I am also creating specific financial goals, which is totally new behavior. I recently heard, 'If you fail to plan, you plan to fail.' With specific goals, I have something to work toward. Failing to set goals is like going to the airport and just getting on any plane, not caring where the plane was going. Who would do that?

"I've also attended 12-Step meetings that focus on money issues and I have sought advice from people who are financially secure so I can become more financially literate. Today I am able to set clear goals to give myself clear direction.

"Where will all of this take me? Honestly, I have no idea, but I do have hope. The most important piece of this is my willingness to change. I have used my anxiety and fear as motivators to do things differently. Let the journey begin!"

Why Did I Keep Doing That?

"I believe we are imprinted at a very early age with specific directions about how to navigate life; as a child I saw how my mother experienced her financial situation, and I reacted accordingly. When my mother felt afraid, I also felt fear. Here was my mother, a god of my life as my parent, feeling dread and panic. If this hugely powerful force in my life felt fear, then it seemed reasonable that I should as well. I naturally took on that panic. As I grew up, I began to compartmentalize the panic and shove it away so I wouldn't have to feel that fear. I ignored my financial life because it was such a source of fear and dread. I had developed no useful tools for the effective management of my money."

My Suggestions for Change

"It is impossible to move to point B if you do not know exactly where you are at point A. So the first piece of counsel I would give anyone walking in my old shoes is to do the work that it takes to get clear about what your financial habits are now.

"Second, I would suggest getting support. If you have serious financial problems I encourage you to explore the 12-Step group Debtors Anonymous. If your problem is not as extreme, hire a trustworthy financial advisor. It is so much easier to go through it with someone else, than to do it alone.

"I would advise you to welcome your financial life into your spiritual life, however you conceive it. I have invited my God into my financial life and I have seen positive results. My relationship to money has changed and I experience real serenity now instead of that old ever-present, nagging anxiety that accompanied any financial choice I had to make in the past.

"Finally, I would suggest that you breathe and relax."

Getting Help

When I was in college at Catholic University in Washington, D.C., a priest friend pointed out to me that my life was a mixed bag of incredible highs and horrible lows. He asked me, "If I foot the bill, will you see a psychiatrist?" I was about seventeen at the time. I said "yes" and the report that came back after two sessions was that I needed professional help right away. So to my parents' surprise, but with their love and support, I began a wonderful journey that continues to this day—discovering who I am and the purpose of my life.

I'm on record as one who loves therapy—not everyone does—and I have been blessed over the years by having some very supportive therapists. At times it was necessary for me, and at other times I probably continued my therapy as a learning experience. Therapy has helped me be what I am and do what I do.

To understand more about the value of therapy and medication, I talked with Dr. Peter D. Kramer.

Peter D. Kramer, M.D.

IS IN PRIVATE PRACTICE IN PROVIDENCE, RHODE ISLAND,
AND IS CLINICAL PROFESSOR OF PSYCHIATRY AND
HUMAN BEHAVIOR AT BROWN UNIVERSITY. HE IS THE AUTHOR OF
THE BESTSELLING BOOKS, *LISTENING TO PROZAC, SHOULD
YOU LEAVE?, MOMENTS OF ENGAGEMENT, AGAINST
DEPRESSION* AND *SPECTACULAR HAPPINESS.*

Dr. Kramer explains:

"In the ordinary course of life, most people find themselves doing things and wondering, 'Why am I doing this? On a rational basis, I have no intention of doing it, and yet I find myself doing it repeatedly.' That's a very common human experience; it's one that the ancient Greek philosophers and Freud worried about, and it's one that neurobiologists think about as well.

"Today there is a range of social classes and a diverse group in therapy—people with major mental illness, people in pain, some looking for an educational experience, some who have achieved great success but still feel unfulfilled.

"Nowadays, there's a great divergence of opinion about the role of medication in psychotherapy. Some people who would have sought out psychotherapy in the past are now only looking for medication. I like to try psychotherapy alone without medication as a first step. Many people get better quite rapidly with psychotherapy by itself. However, if the treatment requires medication, there is no reason not to introduce it fairly early in the process so that there's some hope of creating synergy between the medication and the psychotherapy.

"In some people, the main effect of antidepressants seems to be enhancing self-esteem and building confidence. In others, depression is diminished but they don't automatically feel more self-confident. Still others feel less impulsively angry. We don't really know why these effects vary from person to person. In general, the notion of using psychotherapy with medication is premised on the belief that if you can relieve some aspect of what troubles people, you can sometimes expand that effect by having clients act in a way that gets them some social support and some level of self-understanding.

"If people feel more comfortable within their skin, they're less likely to do desperate things. Medication can also give people a sense of confidence and the wherewithal to manage the catastrophic emotions they're likely to feel during their psychotherapy.

"Most people attempt to accomplish change on their own and come relatively late to either self-help groups or mental healthcare providers. You see everything from people who say, 'I decided to give up smoking and I woke up in the morning and never touched a cigarette again,' to people who are using the patch, taking Wellbutrin, participating in a support group, and *still* thinking about cigarettes all day.

"Psychotherapy ought to respect people and should start with the assumption that clients have some sense of not only what is best for them, but what is consonant with their sense of their own dignity. The real basis for psychotherapy is a deep form of courtesy."

Meet Ben, a Philadelphia commercial real estate salesman who became addicted to work. Workaholism, like busyness, is one of the "accepted" addictions. People who work ten, twelve, fourteen hours daily and see perfect job attendance and not taking vacations as a badge of honor are anesthetizing their feelings just as the drug addict does. It just looks better. Therapy helped turn Ben's life around.

Ben's Compulsion: Work

"I had always thought of myself as a hard worker, someone who was industrious and a model for what a man in our society should be. I worked intensely—'extremely focused' was how some people described me—with a certain intense quality that wasn't always pleasant but that got the job done. I worked long hours, telling myself that I had to achieve certain job-related goals if I were to think of myself as successful. I eschewed vacations as incompatible with my fast-track life, although I envied the time that others spent away from the office having fun. I told myself that I wouldn't do this forever, although I had done it for a long time.

"If my life had been full or emotionally satisfying, I would never have worried, but it wasn't. With each new job and each new city— moving higher in my organization—I was increasingly aware that something was missing, and I told myself that I needed to lead a more balanced life. Yet, I kept doing the same thing despite pleas from my family and friends. When I was away from work trying to have 'fun,' I thought about how much I could be getting done at the office. What had seemed so attractive to me as an activity when I agreed to participate, suddenly became boring compared to my work experience.

"My wife and kids complained about not seeing me, although not about the money that supported our rather affluent lifestyle. Gradually, however, the rewards of my frenetic activity were less and less satisfying. My life was empty, devoid of emotional or spiritual satisfaction, and I began to hurt deeply within. I tried to work less, but I felt guilty and discontented when I wasn't working, and I couldn't focus on the 'fun' I was supposed to be having. When my first child graduated from high school, I realized that except for going to his baseball games, which I had done religiously, I hadn't really been a part of his life. His uncle had. His uncle taught him to drive, helped him do his homework, counseled him when he was unsure about dating—all the things that I should have done. I realized that my boy was much closer to his uncle than to me, and I was jealous of their relationship.

"Despite my efforts, however, I couldn't work less. When I realized that I was doing the same thing over and over, I finally sought the advice of a psychiatrist. It was not easy to give up my hard-work syndrome, but with professional help, I was able to do so. It was painful and scary but it saved my life. Actually, it gave me a new life. I emerged from my cardboard character as worker into a three-dimensional life as a man who was imperfect, but effective at work and at home and at play. By the time my youngest son graduated from high school, I had been there for all the important events of his life. They turned out to be some of the most important events of mine as well."

Why Did I Keep Doing That?

"In my therapy, which was both life-changing and rewarding, I came to realize that my 'hard work' was really compulsive behavior that took me away from two things I had never wanted to face: my inability to feel emotions, and an examination of who I was as a person and a man. The 'hard work' had not been a contribution to society, but the driven work of avoidance. It was not a sense of heightened responsibility that drove me to long hours at the office, but a fear of responsibility—of being responsible for who I was, what I was doing, and how I needed to change."

My Suggestions for Change

"Workaholism is an insidious illness or condition. Seek out professional help. You need it."

I am not quite sure if I like the often-heard therapeutic analogy of peeling the layers of the onion, but I will say without shame, therapy over the years has been very, very meaningful to me. Because of the very positive experience with my psychiatrist when I was a teenager, I guess I have never been shy about asking for help. I have been blessed with having several priests as spiritual advisors and friends. I've had successful mentors in the business world guiding and pushing me. I've read a ton of self-help and inspirational books, have participated in exciting personal growth workshops and seminars, and continue to attend support group meetings with other recovering alcoholics and addicts.

As a television host and author, I've researched and interviewed many of the leading figures in the personal growth field. In the process, I've also discovered there is gold on the Internet, including a formula for change suggested by Barbara, an art dealer in New York City.

She told me about her amazing experience with something she called the "Yoga Technique to Break a Habit" that she used to stop smoking. Shortly after Barbara told me her story, a friend of mine told me he had also used the same technique to quit smoking—with the same successful results. A version of it sits on the Internet: "12 Ways to Quit Smoking," from a health section article on www.Indiatimes.com. The website www.quitsmoking.com offers some wonderful quit-smoking articles.

Barbara's Compulsion: Smoking

"I smoked heavily for eighteen years, from the ages of sixteen to thirty-four. Lighting up got me out of bed in the morning, and I was rarely without a cigarette during my waking moments. Smoking basically ran my life, and in exchange for this slavery, I got to perform in a drama of small repetitive actions which apparently provided an aura of glamour: from holding the pack and taking out the cigarette, to lighting up, inhaling, and then—forcibly, slowly, in contemplation, in reverie, or in amusement—blowing out the smoke in rings, a fan, or a stream out the mouth, the nose, or both. Like all smokers, I cherished the ritual, and the irrational attraction to what may qualify as the world's most stupid habit.

"That I smoked might have been my mother's greatest disappointment. A nurse, she sent me pictures of black lungs and tormented me with pleas to stop. I tried to quit a number of times. Once, after six months of being clean, and with no particular stress at hand, I lit up because, I rationalized, the world was completely absurd anyway and it really didn't matter. There were a few other breaks of shorter duration. At one point I came across the 'Yoga Technique to Break a Habit'—the technique, which is folk knowledge, that ultimately led me to freedom.

"According to the technique to change a habit, you have to lose the desire to act in a particular way. The way you lose the desire is to feed your subconscious mind information causing you to dislike the habit. The subconscious mind is said to be prejudgmental, accepting as valid anything you place there. Information gets stored and rises to consciousness when needed.

"You make two lists. One list enumerates all the bad things about the habit. The second lists all the good things that will happen to you when you break the habit. You read both lists once a day. That is all you do. Here are some examples from my lists.

Bad Things about Cigarettes

    1. Stained teeth
    2. Yellow fingers

3. Bad breath

4. Clothes stink

5. Very expensive

6. Lung cancer

7. Shortness of breath

8. Have to smoke outside

9. People think I'm weak

10. Ashtrays filthy

Good Things about Quitting Smoking

1. Feel clean

2. Breathe easier

3. More time

4. Saving money

5. Feel healthy

6. House doesn't smell

7. Skin looks better

8. People admire me for quitting

9. Food tastes better

10. Feeling of freedom

"You do not need to think about breaking the habit. You do not have to guide yourself into controlling your cravings. You live normally, indulging as you wish in the evil you are attempting to expunge. There is absolutely no forcing of the will, there is no guilt or blame or any other consideration required. All that is required is that you read the lists each day and then go about your usual business. Effort and resolve would certainly not hurt, but they are not required. All you are doing is storing information. It is very simple.

"Of course, just remembering to read the lists can be a challenge. I would forget for weeks at a time, returning sporadically over a period of two years. Then there was a severe physical trauma in my life, and I got very weak. I went from doctor to doctor, but apparently there was nothing physically wrong with me. They couldn't identify a problem, much less offer a solution. Finally, I went to a homeopathic physician. The doctor, a soft-spoken man of very few words, concluded our visit without finding anything wrong with me as well. Almost as an afterthought, however, he asked 'Do you smoke?' I said 'Yes.' He said 'Well, stop smoking.'

"In that very instant my life changed. Suddenly all of the information about smoking, which I had been placing into my subconscious mind, kicked in, spurred on by the homeopath's gentle admonition. I walked out of his office, and never smoked another cigarette. I never wanted a cigarette again. The desire was simply gone, and I mean gone absolutely. Smoking was removed from my existence with no decision on my part, no deliberation, no resolve, and the habit simply evaporated. I had a new life; it was like a miracle, and that was twenty-five years ago.

"Since then, I have never once thought about smoking again. This simple technique changed my life."

Why Did I Keep Doing That?

"I picked up the smoking habit as a teenager doing something that cool people do and I smoked almost through my thirties because it felt good. I loved the ritual of getting out the pack, taking the cigarette out of the pack, preparing it to light, getting out the matches or lighter, putting the cigarette to my lips, lighting, inhaling, holding, exhaling, relaxing, smiling, watching the smoke patterns, checking out the scene."

My Suggestion for Change

"If someone wanted to quit smoking, I would advise them to use the 'Yoga Technique to Break a Habit.' The important thing is that there's no effort required, except to read the lists as often as you remember to do it, trying for once a day."

Loss and Anxiety

Just deciding to change isn't enough. Even if change works for a short time, it's easy to return to old negative patterns of behavior. There are predictable reasons we go back to our old ways. First, we cannot envision ourselves or our life without our old behavior, our old friend; and second, all we can focus on is what we are giving up, what is being taken away. The outcome, the future down the road, is unknown. It's the undertow that drags us back to old behavior.

Change necessitates letting go and leaving behind people, places, and things associated with our self-destructive tendencies and behavior. Whatever you are saying "good-bye" to represents a big loss, perhaps a huge part of who you are right now. That loss should not be minimized. It must be accepted and grieved.

It is crucial to know and accept that at times of traumatic loss, which is what significant change represents, it's impossible for the human mind to contemplate anything other than loss, sadness, and anxiety. In the early stages of change, human beings are incapable of looking forward; they can only look backward. It's the way human beings are built. We cannot imagine, fantasize, or believe that life will be better. We are giving up something that, while it may cause us pain and suffering, actually makes us feel good, at least temporarily.

We are changing our routine, stepping out of our comfort zone, and that, in and of itself, creates discomfort, stress, anxiety, and fear. Major change can be so dramatic that those around us will be greatly affected. Because our negative behaviors often mask our true feelings, our primary relationships may be tested severely. Without our props, which disguise who we really are, our raw, unedited, and authentic feelings may come to the surface, and the targets of our anger, depression, and fear will often be those closest to us.

As we muddle through the change process, we may have to radically alter our lifestyle. That may cause us to move to a different place, go back to school, be lonely for a while, cut people loose, stop using credit cards, enter a clinic or hospital, or attend therapy or support group meetings.

Dramatic change often sets in motion a physical, emotional, mental, and spiritual housecleaning. The positive results are greater self-confidence, a larger comfort zone, increased self-awareness and self-acceptance, and a more productive and happy life. What we experience as an end today is actually the beginning of an exciting new adventure that will reward us with benefits beyond our dreams.

Believe me, I have traveled down that dark road. I cannot begin to tell you how bruised, battered, frightened, and hopeless I was when I began my recovery from alcoholism. I got a second shot at life. Words do not come easily to describe how positive it has been on every level—personal, professional, physical, emotional, mental, and spiritual.

I'm an alcoholic—no embarrassment, no guilt, no shame. Millions of Americans, probably one out of seven who drinks, are alcoholics. I consider myself one of the fortunate ones who found recovery and I don't drink anymore.

Human nature being what it is, you may be or probably are seeking some solution to your own compulsion to repeat. You may be asking, "What should I do to change?" I would be looking for an answer too.

However, first, let's consider the stories of the extraordinary people in this book, the problems they faced and the actions they took:

Manuel, who suffered from low self-worth, continues to attend personal growth seminars, utilizes tapes and exercise, and reaches out to friends.

Sue, who was grossly overweight, met with her doctor and got into a bicycle spinning class and trained for, and participated in, long-distance charity rides.

Chris, the pessimist, read *Learned Optimism* and asked her friend for help.

Jeff, who experienced bouts of rage, called a hotline number, saw a counselor, and attended a support group.

Timothy, a chaos addict, worked each weekend on his problem with a friend.

Jane, Pam, and Maggie, who all had relationship problems, sought out therapists.

John, the procrastinator, got help from his colleagues, support from his wife, and is part of a men's group.

Craig, who had money problems, contacted a financial advisor and joined a 12-Step program.

Ben, a workaholic, saw a psychiatrist.

Sam, the alcoholic, checked into a treatment center and then went to recovery meetings.

Barbara, the smoker, used what she calls the Yoga Technique to Break a Habit and saw a physician.

Victoria joined a codependency support group and saw a therapist.

In my last book, *The Miracle of Change,* I compiled a list of the important principles, the common denominators, of change.

The most important suggestion on the list was, and I quote directly from the book:

"Don't attempt major change alone—do it with an ally. If you are going to change, the first step is to get the support of someone—or some people—you can trust. It's probably going to be three steps forward and two backward, so get the help you'll need to successfully make this major transition."

The biggest value of recovery or support groups, having a therapist or counselor, or working on a problem with a friend, confidant, or member of the clergy, is *not* having to do it alone. Being in a room with others who have faced the same demon and won the battle will offer you hope and inspiration. In therapy, counseling, and coaching, you are creating an intimate partnership with a professional who already has a track record for success. Friends, family members, and colleagues can offer the added support you will need to bring about the changes you seek. Prayer, books, tapes, seminars, and sometimes medication can all make the change process smoother and easier as well.

The changes in our lives are the stepping-stones of self-discovery. The big changes we initiate, which call for courage and action, and the changes thrust upon us, which require acceptance and humility, force us to examine the big questions of life: Who am I? What am I doing here? What purpose do I have? Is there a God? Does God care?

As I see it, the purpose of life is to know myself, accept myself, love myself, and forget about myself in service to others and God. My friend Father Ed used to say, "It takes a long time to make a human being. Change is the catalyst for spiritual growth and life is a spiritual journey."

Be good to yourself. *Don't attempt major change alone.* That's not just my thinking. If you review how all of the book's contributors created the changes in their lives, that's their collective experience and advice as well.

Will you get the help you need from someone—other than yourself?

Quite often, experience tells us that readers put books such as this one aside—never to return. I encourage you to trust yourself to press on. The best is yet to come.

CHAPTER NINE

THE BAD NEWS
IS THE GOOD NEWS

The introspection, hope, faith, and action necessary to bring about the changes we seek may be more difficult to find in the high-pressured and intense world in which we live.

The Washington Post ran an article a few years ago when cell phones were catching on. The reporter interviewed people on a beautiful spring day in one of our local parks. He asked a young woman why she was talking on her phone and walking at the same time. Her response was a window to today's hyperpaced reality. She replied, "Just to walk down the street would be boring." Hello! Has technology changed America for better or worse?

The Bad News

To learn more about our ability to bring about personal change in our fast-paced, technologically driven world, I talked with Dr. Stephanie Brown.

———

Stephanie Brown, Ph.D.

IS THE AUTHOR OF TEN BOOKS AND A FOUNDING BOARD MEMBER
OF THE NATIONAL ASSOCIATION FOR CHILDREN OF ALCOHOLICS.
SHE DIRECTS THE ADDICTIONS INSTITUTE IN MENLO PARK,
CALIFORNIA, AND IS CODIRECTOR OF THE FAMILY
RECOVERY PROJECT AT THE MENTAL RESEARCH
INSTITUTE IN PALO ALTO, CALIFORNIA.

I asked her, "What's going on? Where are we going? What's driving all of this?"

"We are living in a country and culture of chaos. Nowadays, people feel anxious if they're not moving, if they're not striving, if they're not producing. Being on the go and trying to achieve takes people outside themselves so they don't have to cope with whatever internal anxiety they're feeling. People may feel inadequate. 'There's something wrong with me, or something's wrong if I'm feeling this way, if I'm not strong enough to work so hard, so I need some help. I can't feel relaxed enough on my own, so I'll take something to help me relax.' So they reach for a drink, food, or most commonly a sleeping pill. They need something from outside to help on the inside; it is a cultural phenomenon.

"Malcolm Gladwell, in his important book *The Tipping Point,* describes a social epidemic that occurred when the computer world in Silicon Valley hit a 'tipping point.' At that time, he says, the culture actually started to spin out of control with people operating at a frenzied pace. He observed people in a constant state of motion, believing that they were deficient if they could not work twenty-fours a day and seven days a week.

"It's the same fundamental belief structure that operates in people with addictions. 'If I'm not able to control my drinking, there must be something wrong with me, and I need to work harder to find out what's wrong because I should be able to drink as much as I want. It worked in the past, so why can't I drink as much as I want now?'

"That mindset is pervasive—whether in the technology industry or American life in general: 'What's the matter with me that I need sleep?' 'What's the matter with me that I can't keep going?' 'What's the matter with me that I can't drive my car, talk on the cell phone, work my PalmPilot, eat my lunch, and do my taxes all at the same time?' Some of these frantic lifestyles are bizarre yet imperceptible to those living them. People are pushing themselves to the limit, almost beyond human capacity.

"Our country was founded on the premise of unlimited possibility and the notion of manifest destiny. It was a matter of working hard and moving frontiers. The language of our early history is about pushing limits and, often, seizing control of circumstances and unfortunately others. Success was defined as being able to expand, grow, and produce. And that's what we did. We experienced the Industrial Age and now we're in the Age of Knowledge. It's all about limitless technology. Along with that comes a reinstatement of this American dream. So, it seems that some of our history, 'progress,' and subsequent changing values actually fuel negative and repetitive behavior.

"If technology is limitless, how do humans cope? It ignites the old dreams that any of us can have what we want if we work ourselves silly and get lucky. It's a gambling mentality. It's a sweepstakes phenomenon. Drive yourself, be at the right place at the right time, and you'll come out with millions of dollars and you can retire early. Some people do it, so it's not a complete fantasy. On the other hand, how many people destroy their lives in the process? The dream is only for the few. It means chronic failure for the bulk of the population. People hold on to the fantasy and at the end of another twelve-to-eighteen-hour workday, they feel like they've failed. It's an insidious trap. We get swallowed up in all of this work because of the anxiety of being left behind, the anxiety of not having enough, the anxiety of being deprived. There's a bandwagon effect."

Reality Check

Dr. Brown thinks that society can't recognize or acknowledge that we're living and working in an out-of-control culture. So I asked her: "Is there any hope?" She replied:

"People who are too busy are acting out. When the consequences of being out of control begin to stare people in the face, they awaken to the fact that they need limits. With alcohol, it can be a drunk-driving ticket, divorce, or job loss. With the out-of-control culture, it's very similar. We see people getting sick, burning out, going bankrupt, having their business fail, or running up huge debt. Sadly, we also see an increase in children with all kinds of problems because they really don't have parents. The parents are too busy running around believing that the overstimulated life is good. The importance of slow time, down time, being engaged with family and friends, has been lost. The frantic pace can lead to heart attacks and other stress reactions, people seeking medication from their doctors, or the onslaught of excessive drinking, all in the service of people fueling themselves so they can keep up. There are more and more incidents of road rage, and more and more accidents due to distracted drivers talking on their cell phones.

"We're still at that point where people who do manage to get off the treadmill think they've failed. They get depressed and are still blaming themselves. Consciousness raising says, 'Wait a minute, the culture's going to crash. There may be no limits to technology, cyber-space may be unlimited, but humans have limits.'

"The media play an enormous role in our loss of control. The real news isn't enough. It has to be stimulating and exciting and has to capture the emotions of the viewer. That's nuts! The media can behave like the alcoholic family, creating and maintaining chaos to take the focus off the real issues. The culture is in chaos. We're like rats in the cage.

"The problem is that the unrealistic expectations have become the norm, but people are starting to crash into the wall of limits."

If you are feeling burned out, Dr. Brown suggests these questions for your consideration:

> Do you think that life is better or that you are better if you are always on the move?
>
> Is the idea of being able to multitask something you strive for?
>
> Are you finding yourself constantly exhausted or overwhelmed?

Has your life become constant motion, chronic pursuit, no
    end, and no reward?

Do you feel like you're burning out?

Do you think that no matter how much you do, you're failing?

Do you sense that no matter how much you do, it never ends?

If you do stop, do you feel empty?

"The first thing you need to do is break the cycle and trust that it's okay to question your lifestyle. To do that, you will need support. It's hard to get off the merry-go-round by yourself, so you'll need some buddies who are also asking, 'What are we doing here?' A group of people can ask, 'What are we doing, what are our beliefs, what is the price we're paying, is this all there is?'

"When a group of people has a sense of trust, the emptiness becomes a shared emptiness and once you come face to face with the awareness that you're out of control, there will usually be a concerted effort to set limits. Hopefully, at some point, you can say collectively and individually, 'My idea of what I should be doing is wrong. It doesn't work for me. What's been driving me and my belief about what should be possible is the real problem.'"

Human behavior is not two-plus-two-equals-four. There are often no apparent reasons why we do what we do. When we know, however, that something is causing us pain, we should get it out into the light and take a hard look at it.

The simplest explanation for our repeating behaviors, relationships, and feelings—regardless of where they ultimately score on the pain scale—may be as simple as: they feel good!

Satisfaction and Gratification

For more insight into why performing repetitive behaviors often feels good, I talked with Dr. Gerald G. May.

The late Gerald G. May, M.D.

IS THE AUTHOR OF MANY BOOKS, INCLUDING *WILL AND SPIRIT,*
CARE OF MIND/CARE OF SPIRIT, ADDICTION AND GRACE, SIMPLY SANE,
THE DARK NIGHT OF THE SOUL, AND *THE WISDOM OF WILDERNESS.*
A PSYCHIATRIST AND TEACHER, HE WAS A SENIOR FELLOW IN
CONTEMPLATIVE THEOLOGY AND PSYCHOLOGY AT THE SHALEM INSTITUTE
FOR SPIRITUAL FORMATION IN BETHESDA, MARYLAND.

As you continue to read, notice how you will calm down from the frenetic pace described by Dr. Brown to the soothing comfort offered by Dr. May.

"The first thing that comes to mind about repetition is what the behaviorists call conditioning. Our bodies, our minds, our brains have been conditioned to a certain pattern, a certain routine, and when that changes we react and feel like something is wrong. When you multiply that to something that really has a kick in it, like some kind of behavior that has a particularly strong kind of satisfaction—an immediate satisfaction—you can see how that can become more severe, more pervasive, more ingrained, and much more difficult to change.

"That kind of pattern—seeking satisfaction, gratification, and reinforcing behavior around what we now call addiction, compulsion, or obsession—is what the spiritual authorities over the centuries have called attachment. It's the notion, at least in Christian contemplative spirituality, which is my field, that everybody's born with a natural desire for love and fulfillment and, Christians would say, for God. Not knowing any better, we are drawn to the small satisfactions, the good tastes of things, the good feelings that the mystics say are all of God, speak of God, and their goodness comes from God. That's why we like them so much. We're drawn to them and we seek our ultimate gratification from them. Hopping back into modern psychology, what happens through conditioning behavior is we get hooked on those specific things, trying to seek our satisfaction from them."

There is something wonderfully refreshing about labeling our bad habits, addictions, and destructive behaviors as "attachments." Perhaps the attachments concept will help us forgive ourselves for being human.

Dr. May looks at the lure of rewards.

"From a purely psychological standpoint, when there's a behavior that has a reward to it, even if later on there may be negative consequences, that behavior gets reinforced and it's likely to be repeated.

"The more the behavior is repeated, the more reinforcement occurs, the more ingrained the behavior becomes, until you've got a compulsion or an obsession or an addiction that your will or choice or intent can't alter. Everybody has these kinds of behaviors. Some of them aren't what we'd call negative on the surface. They happen subtly, and we only become aware of them in time.

"Here's an example: A person gets his sense of meaning, worth, and value from his work, his productivity. He thinks, if I can succeed enough, I'll ultimately be fulfilled. Or one might want to achieve her ultimate satisfaction through a relationship with a loved one and think that's going to be the answer. We throw ourselves into our work, or this love relationship, or whatever else it might be, all the while establishing conditioned patterns and getting more and more entrenched, only to find out, one way or another, that it isn't going to be our ultimate satisfaction."

Humanness

Dr. May introduces us to the very simplest definition of addiction:

"If there's some kind of behavior or pattern that you want to stop or you'd prefer not to have, and you can choose to stop it and change your ways, that's not an addiction, that's not even a severe attachment. If you can't stop it, well, there you are. That's addiction. That's the definition. It's something you want to stop and you can't.

"We're all addicts. It's difficult to think of something to which we can't get attached. Partly, it's just sheer repetition over and over and over again. For example, we can be addicted to moods or stress or failure. Fundamentally, our nerve cells get used to it. So, if we have some kind of emotional pattern and it repeats itself enough, it becomes part of who we are.

"When I was practicing psychotherapy, one of the common issues that I encountered in working with people with self-defeating behaviors was, when they got to a point where there was understanding of what was going on and enough clarity about what needed to be changed, suddenly great anxiety came up.

"The clients often thought, 'My gosh, if I let go of this pattern, if I stop continually feeling bad about myself, who would I be?' It's like losing part of your identity. While, on the one hand, there may be a great desire to let go of behaviors or attitudes that are unpleasant and self-defeating, on the other hand, right along with it, comes this feeling of 'Oh my gosh, will I even be me?' It's a withdrawal symptom. It doesn't show up until one really begins to realize or approach the possibility of being free—and that can be very scary.

"You can't avoid coming face to face with your own demons, and often we fall back into our repetitive behaviors. Being very tough on ourselves not only brings on self-preoccupation, it also leads to a kind of despair and an empty hopelessness. It can lead to a kind of pattern, a new addiction of 'Oh, I'm such a horrible person.'

"If one's going to make headway, compassion for oneself—a kind of gentleness or tenderness about recognizing our weaknesses and not getting bent out of shape or beating on ourselves—is called for. We have to realize that our addictions, compulsions, and obsessions go along with being physically embodied, being human.

"The Christian mystics are all of one voice and you can see it in all religious traditions. They say that when you fall into some behavior that you don't like or something you consider sinful or bad, you'd best not get into a lot of self-recrimination about it, but simply look to God.

"Julian of Norwich, who lived in the twelfth century, said to God, 'I really wish you would have let me know where I was going to fall. I really would have liked to have known that. But not knowing it, when I fall, all I can do is look to you and get up and take the next step.' Thomas Kelly, the twentieth-century Quaker, when he was consistently trying to be attentive to his interior light said, 'When I stumble, I just look to God and raise my hands and say, "See, this is how I am," and then move on.'

Denial

Dr. May offers some scientific thoughts on addiction:

"Addictions happen because nerve cells, neurons, make physical changes in keeping with behavior and they don't relinquish those changes too easily. When you have something that's a significant attachment, obsession, compulsion, or addiction, you've got a powerful array of nerve cell functioning that keeps that addiction going.

"If you look at addictions neurologically, you can say that the power of the patterns of nerve cell activity that want to keep the addiction going is always greater than the power of the patterns of nerve cell activity that want to stop it.

"It's precisely because of this neurological imbalance that happens in addiction or attachment that we just can't choose on our own to quit the behavior.

"Part of our resistance to ask for help is that factor of addiction that wants to keep things going. Now, just when you're getting a glimpse that you might really be able to give this up, all the subterfuges come in to say, well, you don't really want to give something up.

"One of the most primitive defenses is denial. You're probably not even thinking about asking for help if you're in denial, because you're saying, 'Well, I don't have a problem,' or 'If I've got a problem, I can handle it.' That's a big mitigation against asking for help. There's also the humiliation. We're supposed to have it all together, and if we've a problem, we're supposed to solve it. There are a million and one factors moving against it. You read about honesty, acceptance, confession, discussion, and repentance. You know it will work, and of course you don't want to do it."

The Good News

Dr. May probes the spiritual dimension of freedom from our attachments:

"It is precisely because of all that, that we need to look for something beyond ourselves for help. Maybe it might be a group, or some friends, or counseling. A program where there are brain cells in other people who are willing to align themselves with the part of us that wants to quit is like bringing in reinforcements. Of course, the Divine, the Higher Power, that's the real cavalry coming down the mountain. When that comes, the liberation really happens. If we can't do it on our own then, it just only makes sense that we'd need to turn beyond ourselves wherever we can to try to find some help.

"A lot of people's sainthood, saintliness, or spiritual growth comes out of these addictions. Most of the mystics and spiritual giants that I read will attest to that. Most human beings are so bullheaded—I know I am—I'm not going to let go and let God in until I'm darned sure I can't do it myself, any way I want to.

"The two Christian mystics who I think are the best in the psychological-spiritual arena are Teresa of Ávila and John of the Cross, sixteenth-century Spanish mystics. From my understanding of them, I believe they would say that we're always on a spiritual journey, no matter what we're mired in, no matter how preoccupied we are, no matter what false gods we make for ourselves. We're still all seeking God, and God is seeking us. As the 12-Step people talk about it, maybe we're brought to our knees. Maybe we hit rock bottom and that's when God can reach through and make a difference. Each, in our own way, some more dramatically than others, some more tragically than others, is seeking this ultimate satisfaction. I wouldn't say you couldn't move ahead in the spiritual life when you're mired down in addiction, but it certainly is a lot less pleasant way to be moving.

"Now, there are certain areas of everybody's life where there are particular gifts of grace, and freedom just comes naturally and everything's wonderful. But we've also got all this other buried ugliness in ourselves, and we're bound and determined we're going to handle, or deal with, or cope with, or fix it.

"When the way we are doing things doesn't work and keeps on not working, we reach an impasse. Yet, that's where the hope is, that's where breakthroughs can happen.

"Contemplative hope is vague. It isn't, 'Oh, I hope that by tomorrow I will have cut down on my cigarettes by half.' It's not specific like that, because you learn pretty quickly that those hopes don't pan out. The hope gets simpler and simpler and simpler. Hope for recovery is pretty simple. Maybe it gets even simpler still. 'I just hope to live,' and then, finally, at some point, what it really gets to is, 'I just hope,' without any particular object to that. It goes along with that rock-bottom kind of experience.

"With the severe suffering that addictions can bring us to, the simpler the hope becomes, the more space there is for real freedom. The more we are brought to our knees, the more possibility there is for liberation. That's not a pleasant way to be thinking about it, but I really think it's true. When you use the term slavery applied to addiction, the idea of liberation is a nice counterpoint.

"The good news is the bad news is the good news. We can't handle it, we can't deal with these things, and it's precisely because we can't that some of the deepest surrenders and openings and lovingness are possible.

"If you start with the assumption that the mystics have, that we are all born with a desire for God, desire for ultimate satisfaction, to love and be loved, and that we try to fill that desire with all these things, which wind up to be attachments, then, quite simply, as we are liberated, we are increasingly open and available to what we've really longed for all our lives, for the ultimate satisfaction.

"As St. Augustine said, 'God is always trying to give us good things, but we've got our hands so full of other things that we have no room to receive them.' John of the Cross says, 'The human being has an endless, bottomless capacity for God.' Yet, we fill up that opening for God with all this other stuff. Only when we let go of that 'stuff,' can what we've really been seeking all along come through and the love that we've been looking for can really be realized. That's what it's all about."

Plato wrote, "The unexamined life is not worth living." It's a part of human nature—perhaps one of our basic drives—that people want to grow, change, and be happier. While mega-events do happen, the truth is, life is change. Repeating major problems that sometimes get in the way of a life worth living needs extra special attention. Some of these behaviors and actions fall under the heading of the compulsion to repeat.

CHAPTER TEN

BEYOND THE REPETITION COMPULSION

What drives humans? Why do we do what we do? Why do we engage in self-destructive behaviors? We've almost completed our "menu of possibilities." However, here are a few more intriguing possibilities. They come from a fascinating study by Sylvia L. Teitelbaum, M.S.W., entitled "The Curative Aspects of Repetition Compulsion," published in a 1994 volume of *Contemporary Psychotherapy Review.*

Ms. Teitelbaum writes, "Freud advanced at various times these three theories: 'Action replaced memory, thereby protecting the patient from awareness of his/her past experience;' 'suffering . . . was inherently pleasurable;' and 'the repetition compulsion had its beginning in a derivative of the death instinct.'"

Psychiatrist W. Ronald Fairbairn, M.D., Ms. Teitelbaum says, had another interpretation that focused on relationships: "If there is repeated attachment to inappropriate love objects (where the love objects mirror early attachments), then there is need to renew the devotion to those early ties. Central to human motivation is a profound need for an emotional bond with another. The emotional bond, therefore, is a reconnection to an early love object that may have been malevolent, depressed, or enraged."

Fred Pine, Ph.D., she says, suggests yet another explanation of repeating relationships: "It is a means of holding on to the love object, even if this connection is built mainly around bad experiences. Indeed, even the depressed patient may seek a depriving relationship as the fantasy of a sense of connection with the unavailable love object of the past."

Ms. Teitelbaum concludes with the explanation of the repetition compulsion by Ralph R. Greenson, Ph.D., that ties things up simply: "belated attempts at happy endings to past traumas and frustrations."

Some of the many explanations of the repetition compulsion examined throughout the book—contemporary theories on the compulsion to repeat—may have struck nerves with you. There may be an idea or two into which you may want to dig deeper. Poke around and see what you come up with. For now, with a greater appreciation and respect for the complexity of human behavior, we can be kinder to ourselves when we fail to break bad habits, banish negative feelings, or leave a relationship that diminishes our self-worth.

Dr. Scott Twentyman told us early on, "Much of our life is outside of conscious awareness." That idea alone should encourage us to be less critical and more forgiving of ourselves and others when we stumble. When we try to change and move out of our comfort zone, we may very well fall. Like a baby, we are learning to walk. When the baby falls, the baby doesn't quit. The baby gets up and tries to walk again.

You've met some extraordinary people—like you—who have brought about change in their lives. Here is a list of ways they've achieved their goals:

Crisis

Therapy, analysis, counseling, and coaching

Support groups

Intense emotional experiences

Self-discipline and personal effort

Friends or family

Growth seminars

Prayer

Medication

Books, lectures, tapes, television shows, articles, and videos

Exercise

A miracle

A prime requisite for change, of course, is courage. Change, by its very definition, provokes fear. The greater the change, the greater the fear. The status quo, our security, is threatened. Change necessitates that we move into an unknown emotional environment, and that creates anxiety. Courage is taking action in the face of fear. If you wait to conquer the fear, the change will never happen. You've got to acknowledge the fear and plow through it.

Along with courage, perhaps we should add humility as a prerequisite for change. Humility is the willingness to ask for help and to learn. The people in this book who have successfully conquered their own compulsion to repeat say that the more outside support they utilized, the faster and easier it was to achieve success.

Follow your own path in getting where you want to go; however, take advantage of whatever help is available. Don't try to accomplish major change alone; it's the hard way, and help is just a phone call away. If you really are serious about change, reach out. The success you want may escape you if you try to go it alone.

Making a decision to move forward requires setting a goal, and it's best to do that in writing. Make a contract with yourself to achieve your goal in a reasonable amount of time. Tell your inner circle what you are trying to do and ask them for their support. And give yourself credit for even making the commitment to begin the change process.

Motivational speaker and writer, businessman and marketing genius Harvey Mackay told me, "A goal is a dream with a deadline. It is measurable, identifiable, attainable, specific, and should be in writing. Pale ink is better than the most retentive memory, which means, write your goals down."

The following questionnaire may help.

First Steps to Change

What is the behavior, relationship, or feeling causing your struggle? _____

_____

_____

_____

Honesty: In what way are you responsible for the problem?

_____

_____

_____

Willingness: Are you really committed to stopping this behavior now? _____

_____

_____

_____

Commitment: Will you make this important change your top priority for at least ninety days? _____

_____

_____

_____

Action: What immediate actions will you take to make this happen? _____

_____

_____

_____

Courage: What is your biggest fear? Will you take action in the face of it? _____

_____

_____

_____

Humility: Will you ask for help? Who will you ask? _____

_____

_____

_____

_____

Faith: Do you believe in the success of others being able to change? _____

_____

_____

_____

Some runners log every mile on a personal calendar, which they keep specifically for that purpose. Some people who are dieting chart their weight every day. Keep a daily record of your progress. Write in a daily journal and acknowledge your fears and anxiety about making this major change. Keep telling yourself that the fear and anxiety are normal and human. Others have survived those feelings, and you will too.

Affirmations can be helpful, too. Write them out and keep them visible—for example, "I will be on time for my appointments and commitments. Being on time makes me feel good about myself, and I will experience those positive feelings." Try to substitute some new behavior that makes you feel good physically and emotionally about yourself. Exercise almost always seems to help.

Inner Conflict

Have you identified the inner conflict driving your negative behavior? The symptom is the conscious manifestation of what is really going on deep down inside. Remember the symptom is the obvious problem. It is relieving the anxiety of a deep inner conflict, but it's also creating more stress.

What is the inner conflict manifesting itself through your symptom? _____

_____

_____

Understanding alone is the booby prize. Use that important insight to really move your life forward.

Remember, until significant progress has been made in the change process, it is almost "normal" for the smoker to reach for a cigarette, the workaholic to begin a new project at quitting time, and the rejected partner to attempt to rekindle romance with the lover who has just ended their relationship.

Vulnerability to the undertow—reverting back to old negative patterns—is to be expected. Vigilance is the key to success.

One of the most important things I learned in my therapy with Tarpley Long was that some of the deeper issues we tackle never go away completely. I've learned that I am still vulnerable to slipping back into old negative patterns in certain situations or with certain people. When those situations present themselves, I've learned to "buy time," evaluate the situation, and make healthier choices instead of self-destructive ones. I have been especially well trained to pay attention to that vulnerability when I am lonely, overly tired, angry or resentful, hurt, feeling insecure, or hungry.

Vulnerability

Dr. Robert Johnson has some important thoughts on this topic of vulnerability.

"Repeating behaviors are a part of life. Many of these learned behaviors are neither entirely negative nor positive. When someone has a feeling or thought unattached to a specific action, it is a private experience and nothing to feel particularly guilty about. Our thoughts should be fun, enjoyable; it's one of the nice things we have as human beings. But you'd be surprised how many people come to therapy who feel terribly guilty about their thoughts.

"Learned behaviors are so ingrained that people constantly have to think about them to avoid them. At our weakest moments there is often no energy to focus on the process of thinking, so you slip up and repeat the behavior. When we're really tired or worried, we rely on a lower order of thinking—automatic responses rather than responses that require a great deal of thought. At those times, the energy required to break a severe habit or a negative pattern of behavior is often not available to produce or maintain change.

"Adverse behaviors are more likely to appear at times of sadness, anger, or hurt. These feelings can reduce or even prevent the mental energy it takes to overcome a repetitious behavior. When a wife says something upsetting to her husband, he knows he should not say anything, but his mental resistance is low because he's tired, and so he blows up. Once that happens, it's too late. It's probably not a new argument they're having, and now he wants to kick himself for losing control in that moment of weakness.

"It may be impossible to avoid saying something harmful when you're tired or hurt, but before that point occurs, it may be possible to control the circumstances that are going to lead to the breaking point. People can start to control the things associated with resurfacing negative behavior and begin to break the vicious cycle.

"Examine the last time you got into a fight. Reflect on the circumstances and the things that led up to it. What happened an hour before you blew up that caused the argument? You can't control things two minutes before a blow up, but you may be able to control things an hour before that critical point, when you're in a better position to act differently, when you have more positive energy, and when you're better able to say other things.

"Hurt probably provokes the greatest vulnerability. If you can identify the trigger that can prevent hurt, you're way out in front. When we are hurt by someone or something, we become sad and fatigued and are more than likely to lose control over the trigger, and we may repeat some repetitive behavior to solve/cure the hurt—such as eating a half-pint of Häagen-Dazs, taking a drink, or going on a shopping spree."

Be Prepared

Dr. Johnson says that anticipation and preparation may defuse a potential relapse into old repeating patterns.

"Say you're going to a party with a date for the first time. You know that if she rejects you, then you're going to be hurt, and once you're hurt you're going to get angry or depressed and have more than a couple of drinks. You accept the vulnerability you may have in this situation. Then you pause and think, 'What are the things I can do to prevent this? I can either not meet her at all, I can find out from someone else whether she's likely to respond positively to me, or I can arrange the date to be with other friends so that, if it doesn't work out and I do feel hurt, I can shift my focus to enjoy being with them.'

"You can begin to manipulate the circumstances in such a way that you can mitigate the possibility that the adverse behavior will occur. With some creative thinking, you can analyze how to handle a stressful situation with your boss as well. It requires a relatively high degree of cognitive ability, but it's possible. It's one of the techniques I use frequently. What I'm suggesting is:

See a repeating behavior.

Do some analytical thinking about it.

Realize that there's an area of vulnerability where it may rear its ugly head.

Be prepared to act upfront before you get to the crossroads.

Don't beat yourself up for getting into that trap again.

"You may or may not have the ability to stop because you simply can't, but what you can control are some of the circumstances that lead you up to that critical point."

Is it possible that we have been so negatively programmed for failure and unhappiness as children that a primary reason for our unhappiness as adults is a fear of feeling happy, being joyful, being successful? The answer may be "yes."

The Comfort of Familiarity

Why do we keep putting our hand back in the fire when we know certain situations, behaviors, and relationships cause us pain and suffering?

To find out why, I asked Dr. Stella Resnick.

Stella Resnick, Ph.D.

IS A PSYCHOLOGIST IN PRIVATE PRACTICE IN LOS ANGELES.
SHE IS A PAST PRESIDENT OF THE WESTERN REGION
OF THE SOCIETY FOR THE SCIENTIFIC STUDY OF SEXUALITY
AND THE AUTHOR OF *THE PLEASURE ZONE*.

Dr. Resnick says that familiarity is comforting because it's automatic and so it feels easy. When we apply that yardstick to our repeating negative behaviors, the implication is that some of us are actually comforted by pain. That's a very difficult truism for a lot of us to grasp or accept.

Dr. Resnick brings our investigation in this book full circle: Many of us feel good, feeling bad.

"We tend to keep ourselves going down a very narrow path, almost like wind-up toys. We're wound up to go in a particular direction and we move in that direction. When we hit a wall we just walk backward, then set off again on the same path and hit the same wall. We keep it up even though it hurts, all the time wondering why do I keep hitting the same wall?

"When people continually engage in patterns of behavior which produce pain, it is because we have actually been programmed that way. Research on developing infants shows that how we react to stress has been programmed into the brain and nervous system from our earliest months and years. It's not easy to change our patterns because they are part of the way we are wired. Change is possible but it does take some skill and a willingness to invest ourselves in doing things differently. I have actually heard people say that to act in a more positive and loving way was unnatural for them. They'll say, 'You don't want me to not be myself, do you?' And I'll say, 'Well, if being you is being abusive to yourself or others, then, yes indeed, I'd like to help you be somebody else. I'd like you to help you find a you that is more accepting and more loving.'"

Playing the Victim

"What's the payoff?" Dr. Resnick explains:

"There may be secondary gains or hidden payoffs that propel us to act in ways that perpetuate pain. Some people are attached to seeing themselves as a victim. When we identify as victims, we get a certain kind of sympathy that, when we don't know any better, passes for love. Sympathy is not love, but if we haven't really known true love that is accepting, nurturing, affectionate, caring, supportive, and kind, we'll take whatever we can get—even if it is sympathy. We'll make excuses for our behavior, and we'll take pity. The problem is, pity doesn't satisfy so we keep repeating the victim behaviors in the hope that somehow sympathy or pity will magically transform into genuine love and nourishment. But that doesn't happen. We really need to look at the underlying payoff and whether the payoff is a counterfeit for the real thing."

You Can't Get There from Here

Dr. Resnick says that if we act in a negative way, we're going to end up with a negative result. She often tells her clients, "Where you want to go, you can't get to from here."

"Does your behavior bring you what you want? I tell people, 'You say you want love; well, screaming and yelling are not going to make anybody love you. 'You can't get there from here.' Who told you that's the way to be? Where did you learn that if you work hard day and night and have a big house and a fancy car that will bring you love and happiness? Have you seen that to be the case or is it something you just tell yourself? All you know to do is to stay focused on accumulating wealth or getting the accolades of others. Suddenly you find it isn't bringing you what you thought it would. 'This is not making me happy. What do I need to make me happy?'

"Approaching life with a sense of excitement, enthusiasm, adventure, interest, and curiosity, or approaching life with fear, shame, hiding, or trying to get by is learned. When we tell ourselves that life is difficult, that we won't be loved, that we don't deserve to have what we want, that promotes contraction, restriction, and feelings of heaviness. It stops us from moving forward to embrace life. We find ourselves motivated more by avoiding pain than by embracing joy and pleasure. We're just concentrating on avoiding the pits in the road. We're looking down and we're not seeing what lies ahead, the possibilities that exist. That takes a certain trust.

"Some people are focused on the negative because they think anticipating worst-case scenarios is the way to avoid catastrophe. I'm fond of telling people: 'You may not live long enough for your worst expectations to come true.' If we grow up thinking this is a dangerous world, a hostile universe, then those negative thoughts create pain and contraction inside of us, and that pain and contraction make us act in negative ways. Pain is contagious. If you walk into a room and everybody is feeling anxious, how long is it before you feel anxious? If you walk into a room and everybody is feeling loving and warm, pretty soon you will feel loved, comfortable, and loving.

"I think we have a tendency in our culture to focus on the negative. If we don't have a balanced life, if we don't get our pleasure from work, relationships, solitude, children, animals, physical activity, sexuality, and playfulness—if we don't get a full range of pleasures, then, whenever we allow ourselves some little pleasure, it's hard to set boundaries. In our hunger, we overdo things. We can't get enough so we end up paying the price for starving ourselves in the first place."

According to Dr. Stella Resnick, the process of change can begin simply. Living a happy life, she says, requires experimenting with new ways of doing things.

"When I want to help people do something differently, I don't ask them to change. I ask them to experiment by doing things a little differently—even having fun with adopting a new approach to an old situation.

"A man with whom I was working would get in his car in the morning, and as he drove to work he would think about all the things that could go wrong at the office. By the time he got to the office, he was tense and not looking forward to the day. For awhile, we worked on getting him to think about the good things that he could encounter, but he would very easily lapse into thinking about the bad things.

"So I said to him, 'Okay, I'd like you to give yourself the permission to consciously think of the worst things you can encounter. Consciously do it, not by default, but choose it. Choose to think the worst. During the first half of your commute give yourself permission to think the *worst* and really get into it. Then, give yourself equal time to counter all your negative expectations with positive ones and think about the *best* things that could happen.' That worked for him and he was amazed. By giving himself permission to think the worst, he actually took conscious control over something he was doing automatically. It's called 'negative practice,' an old term in psychology that was used originally with people who stutter. Instead of trying to get people who stutter to stop stuttering, you teach them how to stutter consciously. You teach them to take conscious control over an undesired behavior by becoming aware of what it is that they are doing so that they can do something different. I use 'negative practice' for people who have habits that they can't seem to break. It may feel silly at first, but negative practice enables people to get conscious control over unproductive behavior so that they can *choose* to do things in a more fulfilling and more productive way."

Avoiding Pleasure

According to Dr. Resnick, we need to be very clear about what we want, where we want to go, and how we want to live. She encourages us to evaluate whether our behaviors are bringing us what we say we want and whether our ways of thinking, acting, and feeling ever brought us the kind of positive results we say we want for ourselves.

"Can people be trapped repeating negative behaviors as a way of avoiding pleasure? Absolutely! They're afraid that if they allow themselves a little pleasure, they'll open the floodgates to shameful behavior. When people lack familiarity with letting themselves enjoy positive energy, then they control, control, control. Suddenly, they can't control anymore and they do something that's self-destructive.

"The flip side of punishment is pleasure. When you talk about pleasure, many people think you're promoting self-interest and self-ishness—that you're going to step all over everybody, use other people for your own purposes, and be insensitive to other people's needs because you're in it only for yourself. That makes no sense at all. If you act like a complete bore and you're only interested in yourself, who the hell is going to want to be with you? If nobody wants to be with you, how happy are you going to be all by yourself?

"Pleasure propels you to explore your world. It's about moving forward, toward what gives you open, warm feelings as opposed to pain, which blocks you. Pleasure is expansive. Pain is constrictive. Pain makes us close off, makes us avoid; pleasure makes us open—it gives us the energy to move forward. Pleasure is a physiological state, not just a psychological one, and it generates the enthusiasm to create and grow.

"We need to expand our horizons, to experiment, to try new things. We need to have more of a sense of adventure with and in life. If you're doing things differently—even when it brings pleasure—the new, unfamiliar behavior will feel uncomfortable at first and you may have a certain resistance to doing it. However, once you start to practice new ways of doing something, you will reap unexpected rewards and the new behaviors will make you feel energetic and courageous. At that point the new behavior begins to have a life of its own."

Dr. Resnick, implores us to slow down, monitor our feelings, and pay attention to what our feelings tell us.

"I call my work Embodied Process therapy and it integrates a somatic-experiential focus into the more traditional cognitive-behavioral approaches. 'Somatic' means that all emotions are based in the body, and 'experiential' means that it's not enough just to examine how you think or act. You can learn a lot more about yourself by attending to inner experience. It's very important that we look more deeply into the body, into how thoughts create feelings. Take some deep breaths and focus your attention inwardly on how your body feels. Experience the sensations in your body, and pay attention to the thoughts that create those sensations and how it makes you want to act.

"Living a happy life requires continually checking in with yourself, and choosing how you want to do things and not just acting by default according to how you were programmed decades ago. It requires breathing, relaxing, and being in your body so that you can manage your stress effectively and be in touch with your deepest feelings, your deepest urges, and your highest dreams."

Father John Powell, S.J., wrote a terrific little book, *Why Am I Afraid to Tell You Who I Am?* My own answer to his question centers on avoiding rejection and seeking approval. That may be the more honest answer from many actors, performers, and people in the public eye. For politicians and business executives, throw in control and power as well. From the time I was doing magic tricks in the living room as a kid to my adult career as a television interviewer and author, some of my motivation—now clearer to me than ever before—has been seeking approval.

Dale Carnegie says in *How to Win Friends & Influence People,* "Get people to talk about what interests them." It's a positive thought. I have followed that suggestion professionally to build a successful career; however, personally I may have used that to actually hide who I am, what I feel, what I want, what I need, what I like and dislike, what I am for or against.

In all things? Of course not, but surely in some areas.

My own compulsions to repeat negative behaviors have run the gamut. I have destroyed some very good friendships, sabotaged lucrative business opportunities, and hurt some very caring people. My negative patterns have cost me and others dearly. I sincerely apologize to all who may have been caught in my self-centered wake.

In the past, negative behaviors, feelings, and relationships dictated my life, causing me to act out an often painful, harmful, and self-defeating script that said, *You are not good, you are not lovable, you are not capable, you are not worthwhile, you are not important.* I don't see that as true anymore. I don't live that life.

My friend Philip says: "You are always in your prime." I think that's true. It's a very exciting time for me and I'd rather be me than anybody I know.

A big change process started for me a couple of years ago at a seminar I attended in New York City. I couldn't say at the time how I was being affected, but I knew that something important was happening. Professionally, a more human and more gentle television series became our direction. "This Is America" producer, Jonathan Oglesby, and I have shifted the focus and tone of our series dramatically. While we still produce roundtable discussions, our programs are more informational than confrontational, and many of our weekly shows are one-on-one personal conversations with guests who contribute to our country and the world in a positive way. This year we began producing a second television series, "I Believe," to learn about different religions and faiths—the spiritual side of life.

Personally, my close relationships are now more important to me than ever before, and I am putting more of myself into them. My physical, mental, emotional, and spiritual health is excellent. I am optimistic about the future.

Michigan psychologist Jack Gregory, who helped me a great deal in my early days of recovery, says, "Everything that has happened should have." I have few regrets. I thank my parents, both now deceased, and my sisters and brothers, my extended family, and close circle of friends for their love and support. Over the years, they have cut me a lot of slack. I have been blessed and I have gratitude for the whole package. Let the adventure continue.

It's your turn now to stretch and grow. Get very clear about your passion, what you really want from this life, how you can contribute to others, and what is presently in the way of getting you where you want to go. Find the help you need to break out of the box you got into a long time ago, and make your passion your reality.

I believe that God gave each of us a little job to do. It's our mission to identify that job and do it. If we don't do it, it doesn't get done.

So, what's your passion?

The world does not give us value; it is we who give value to the world. Remember,

> *You're getting what you're getting,*
> *because you're doing what you're doing.*
> *If you don't like what you're getting,*
> *change what you're doing.*

INDEX